Abu Zayd Publishers Ltd

Depression in Muslim adults: Identification and recognition amongst Imams in Leicester, with special reference to creating a pathway of combined cross-sector care.

Mohammed Kolia

Published in the UK by AZ Publishers Ltd, UK.

Printed by Amazon, UK.

ISBN: 9798721421488

Markfield Institute of Higher Education

(Validated by Newman University)

Masters Level Dissertation

Depression in Muslim adults: *Identification and recognition amongst Imams in Leicester, with special reference to creating a pathway of combined cross-sector care.*

Dissertation submitted in partial fulfilment of the requirements for the degree of MA Islamic Studies at the Markfield Institute of Higher Education, validated by Newman University.

Mohammed Owaise Kolia MPharm, MA

Supervisor(s): Dr Ataullah Siddiqui and Dr Zahid Parvez

August 2020

Acknowledgments

In the name of Allah, the Entirely Merciful, the Especially Merciful.

I am grateful to my Lord for the opportunities provided to me, and for every breath that I take. I am grateful to my parents who have supported me throughout, my wife, The Markfield Institute, its teachers, supervisors, administration staff, and the students who have all supported me throughout this project.

I am grateful to the participants of this study who took time out from their schedules for the research.

This work is dedicated to my son Zayd who I pray will be able to exert an influence in the future and help support those suffering from mental health conditions in our communities.

'Service to others is the rent you pay for your room here on earth.'
- Muhammad Ali

Contents

Abstract

Imams play an important role within the Muslim community. The aim of this study is to help us understand how Imams can make a valuable contribution to the identification and recognition of symptoms of Depression. The objective is also to address if Imams can form part of a combined pathway of cross-sector care to deliver better outcomes for those suffering with Depression in our communities. More importantly, the study aims to build on the key recommendations as set out in the report by the independent Mental Health Taskforce to the NHS in England (in their Five Year Forward View) in to how the community, and in specific faith leaders can play a part in the recognition of conditions such as Depression.[1]

Public Health England (PHE), an executive agency of the Department of Health and Social Care (DHSC) has made clear that faith leaders have a role to play in identifying people at risk, yet there has been no guidance in to *how* this can be achieved.[2] This study can go some way to understanding the perceptions of Imams on their role in recognising and supporting people through Depression. The hope is that this allows us to build on the NHS Five year Forward view into mental health, and support the development of a future protocol of combined

---

[1] The Mental Health Taskforce (2016). The Five Year Forward View for Mental Health: A report from the independent Mental Health Taskforce to the NHS in England. [ONLINE] Available at: https://www.england.nhs.uk/wp-content/uploads/2016/02/Mental-Health-Taskforce-FYFV-final.pdf [Accessed 01/10/19]

[2] Public Health England (2016). Local Suicide prevention planning. [ONLINE] Available at: https://assets.publishing.service.gov.uk/government/uploads/system/uploads/attachment_data/file/585411/PHE_local_suicide_prevention_planning_practice_resource.pdf. p.16 [Accessed 01/10/19]

cross sector care involving faith leaders, with inevitably better outcomes for those suffering with Depression.[3]

Whilst we consider Depression epistemologically as a scientific phenomenon, it's interpretation sociologically becomes a double-hermeneutic one,[4] therefore Giddens thesis of the mediation of paradigms between natural science and sociology forms a major part of the theoretical framework of interpretive analysis for this work. Using this philosophical concept, 12 Imams were interviewed in Leicester to explore their perceptions of Depression, and on how their role can impact Muslim Adults in Leicester with respect to their mental health condition.

This was a largely qualitative case study design that focused on coding to set up key themes within the interviews. Magnitude coding and frequency coding were used to contextualise the responses.

Of the 15 Imams that were contacted, 12 responded and agreed to participate in the study. A majority of these Imams were either born here or already settled for over 20 years. On average the Imams had a minimum of 10 years of experience within their roles as Imams. The Imams showed that they were able to recognise signs and symptoms of Depression, and none had attributed these to Jinn possession. 8 out

---

[3] The Mental Health Taskforce (2016).
[4] Psychology today (2013). ADHD and the Problem of the Double Hermeneutic. [ONLINE] Available at: https://www.psychologytoday.com/gb/blog/theory-knowledge/201312/adhd-and-the-problem-the-double-hermeneutic [Accessed 22/03/2020]

12 Imams had not referred at all to any other professional in the last 12 months, though on average at least 9 hours a week were being spent on counselling their congregants.

Imams had acknowledged that women did suffer from not having the support from Imams that their male counterparts would have and a majority of Imams were in favour of greater access and support for women. All the Imams recognised the need for further training on counselling and Depression and were open to cross-collaboration with other professionals.

The study recommends to provide formal RCBT training to Imams, improve access for Muslim women to support through virtual sessions and RCBT trained Aalimas, and to design a protocol of referral based on learnings from safeguarding policies and the e-Referral service to improve cross-sector collaboration.

1. Introduction

In the immediate years following the global financial crisis of 2008, the city of Leicester saw a significant peak in the number of cases of suicide.[5] Between 2008 to 2010, an average of 106 persons per year committed suicide in Leicester, significantly above the national average (of 9.4 per 100,000 population).[6] The suicide count in Leicester in the last ten years has been above the national average in adults (10.5 people per 100,000 population compared to national average of 9.63 people per 100,000 population in the UK).[7] In 2018, there were 6859 deaths that were recorded as suicide in the UK and Republic of Ireland,[8] but there are a significantly larger number of people that are either thinking about suicide, making plans for it, or actively planning it.[9]

To take a proactive effort in to suicide prevention the DHSC produced a progress report in January 2017 based on a national strategy document published in 2012. In it they identified the high-risk groups that required key areas of action. One of the five were **people in the care of mental health services, including inpatients. Whilst this report highlights mental health disorders as a key risk factor for suicide, it**

---

[5] Public Health England. (2018) Suicide prevention profile. [ONLINE] Available at https://fingertips.phe.org.uk/profile/suicide/data#page/0/gid/1938132828/pat/6/par/E12000004/ati/102/are/E06000016 [Accessed 01/10/19]

[6] Ibid

[7] Ibid

[8] Samaritans. (2019) Suicide statistics report. [ONLINE] Available at: https://www.samaritans.org/documents/402/SamaritansSuicideStatsReport_2019_AcMhRyF.pdf. [Accessed 01/10/19]

[9] National Institute for Health and Care Excellence. (2011) Common health problems: Identification and pathways to care. [ONLINE] Available at https://www.nice.org.uk/guidance/cg123/chapter/Introduction [Accessed 13/12/18]

focuses on those that are *already* accessing mental health services and recommends that additional training is needed for staff to improve the identification, treatment and management of Depression in primary care.[10]

Whilst historically major health policy decisions have been informed by mortality rates, the lack of emphasis on morbidity significantly undervalues the exceptionally large number of people that suffer with Depression, and as such this mental health disorder is far more debilitating than suicide statistics suggest.[11] However, because the epidemiology of the condition is poorly understood (to be discussed further in literature review), its *relative* prevalence in relation from one locality to the next can be analysed to some extent through mortality rates (suicide statistics).[12]

The NHS defines Depression as:
'A broad and heterogeneous diagnosis characterised by depressed mood and/or loss of pleasure in most activities. Severity of the disorder is determined by both the number and severity of symptoms and the degree of functional impairment.'[13]

---

[10] HM Government Department of Health and Social Care. (2017) Preventing Suicide in England: third progress report of the cross-government outcomes strategy to save lives. [ONLINE] Available at
https://assets.publishing.service.gov.uk/government/uploads/system/uploads/attachment_data/file/582117/Suicide_report_2016_A.pdf [Accessed 01/10/19]
[11] Whiteford, H. Ferrari, A. et al. (2010) The Global Burden of Mental, Neurological and Substance Use Disorders: An Analysis from the Global Burden of Disease Study. [ONLINE] Available online at:
https://journals.plos.org/plosone/article?id=10.1371/journal.pone.0116820 [Accessed 13/03/20]
[12] Ibid
[13] NICE. (2011) Common health problems: Identification and pathways to care.

The NICE (National Institute for Health and Care Excellence) guidance on common mental health problems states that Depression and anxiety represent the most common forms of mental health disorders. It also states that Depression specifically is associated with high levels of morbidity and mortality and is the most common disorder contributing to suicide.[14]

Following on from the DHSC suicide prevention report, as part of local authority suicide prevention planning strategy, Public Health England has identified that *faith leaders* are one of the stakeholders to engage in a multi-agency approach to mental health, and suicide prevention.[15] In the Muslim community, *Imams* play this role. In a report published by The Muslim Council of Britain (MCB) the typical services offered by mosques, apart from prayer spaces include counselling and family support, supplementary education, youth diversionary projects and holiday programmes.[16] It states that the role of the Imam in British mosques has undergone sweeping changes in the past thirty years in response to the evolving socio-economic needs of the Muslim community: from their humble beginnings as volunteer Imams, to the current day role of teacher, guide, scholar, social worker, counsellor, family mediator, chaplain and community leader amongst other things.[17]

---

[14] Ibid
[15] Public Health England. (2016) Local Suicide prevention planning.
[16] Rahman, S. Ahmed, S. Khan, S. (2006) Voices from the minarets: MCB study of UK imams and mosques. Stratford, UK: Published by The Muslim Council of Britain, pp. 6.
[17] Ibid, pp. 7.

Research has shown that approximately only 35% of adults of all ages seek help for a mental disorder, and the major barriers to seeking help are difficulty in identifying symptoms, lack of accessibility of support services, and concerns about confidentiality and trust (amongst others).[18]

Imams can play a vital role in bridging the divide of perceived barriers to seeking help and getting the help that they need.

Figure 1.1

PHE, Local suicide prevention planning, 2016

---

[18] Jorm, A. (2011). Mental Health Literacy: Empowering the Community to Take Action for Better Mental Health. American Psychologist. [ONLINE] Available at: https://www.semanticscholar.org/paper/Mental-health-literacy%3A-empowering-the-community-to-Jorm/69946b3064897c38d27596d2c4902f431f0dbb67 [Accessed 01/10/19]

As the role of the Imam has developed over time, and as Depression is a major cause of suicide in adults, are Imams equipped to recognise the symptoms? Does there need to be a training programme to highlight any learning needs? Our research proposal aims to look in to two major areas that encompass the questions above, namely;

1.   **Are Imams aware of signs and symptoms of Depression?**

The issue of awareness of signs and symptoms is a pertinent one, as a common reason for people not seeking help with Depression is the difficulty in identifying the symptoms of Depression.[19] The symptoms can often be *accommodated* to be perceived as 'normal' due to a reluctance in wanting to seek help.

2.   **Can a combined cross-sector approach to care be formulated whereby Imams also play a role in the mental wellbeing of individuals alongside other professionals?**

Such a study requires therefore a qualitative research design so that we can explore the attitudes of the Imams in respect the symptoms of Depression. How do Imams *truly* feel about it? And in doing so, we can then gage whether there is appetite for a cross-sector combined approach to care, and what this would look like.

---

[19] Gulliver, A. Griffiths, K. (2010) Perceived barriers and facilitators to mental health help-seeking in young people: a systematic review. BMC Pshyciatry. [ONLINE] Available at: https://bmcpsychiatry.biomedcentral.com/track/pdf/10.1186/1471-244X-10-113 [Accessed 13/03/20]

In an article by The Joseph Rowntree Foundation titled 'The impact of the global economic downturn on communities and poverty in the UK,' Naomi Hossain states that following the downturn (Global Financial Crisis, 2008) people on low incomes had felt the effects of the rising cost of living associated with food and fuel price increases in international markets, and that more effort, time, stress and uncertainty were involved, and more help from friends, family and neighbours was needed to keep households going.[20] The Bank of England has warned that a worst-case Brexit could be more painful for our nation than the global financial crisis,[21] and as we enter in to an uncertain 2020, this may bring added socio-economic uncertainty to many people in Leicester. Furthermore, a survey conducted by the charity YoungMinds during the peak of the Covid-19 pandemic stated that 83% of participants said the pandemic had made their conditions worse and 26% said they were unable to access any mental health support during the crisis.[22] Imams therefore need to be ready to recognise and support with the recognition and identification of Depression in order to bring better quality outcomes for those that are suffering with Depression, or those that are feeling the impact of supporting a family member through Depression.

---

[20] Joseph Rowntree Foundation (2011). The impact of the global economic downturn on communities and poverty in the UK. [ONLINE] Available at https://www.jrf.org.uk/report/impact-global-economic-downturn-communities-and-poverty-uk [Accessed 01/10/19]

[21] The Guardian. (2018) Bank of England says no-deal Brexit would be worse than 2008 crisis.
[ONLINE] Available at: https://www.theguardian.com/business/2018/nov/28/bank-of-england-says-no-deal-brexit-would-be-worse-than-2008-crisis [Accessed 01/12/19]

[22] Mental health effects of school closures during COVID-19. (2020) Available [ONLINE] at: https://www.thelancet.com/journals/lanchi/article/PIIS2352-4642(20)30109-7/fulltext. [Accessed 01/06/2020]

2. Literature review

The literature review focused around:

1. The Clinical Study of Depression
2. Islamic perspective on mental health
3. The role of Imams
4. The Perceptions of mental health amongst ethnic minorities

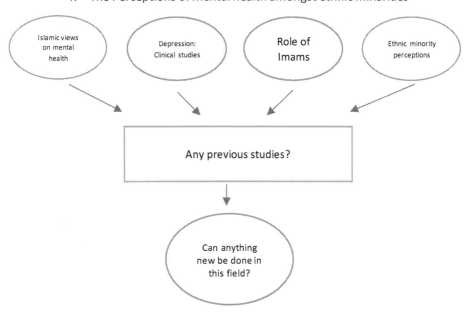

Figure 2.1

Literature review

2.1 Depression

The understanding of Depression historically, as well as now has mostly been understood as either:

- A pathophysiological condition and/or
- A cognitive condition and/or
- A behavioural or spiritual disorder

From a pathophysiological perspective mental health disorders such as Depression are thought to be caused by dysregulation or genetic abnormalities within neurotransmitters that affect brain function.[23] However, there is of yet no credible evidence that mental health disorders are caused *exactly* by chemical imbalances, or no credible biological markers that may validate this, except in theory.[24] This biochemical model is accused of often only playing lip service to cognitive or behavioural theories and treatments, in that it only focuses on a single hermeneutic understanding of the disease, its physiological etymology and treatment.[25] As Dr Paul Appelbaum

---

[23] Deacon, B. (2013) The biomedical model of mental disorder: A critical analysis of its validity, utility, and effects on psychotherapy research. Clinical Psychology Review. [ONLINE] Available at:
https://jonabram.web.unc.edu/files/2013/09/Deacon_biomedical_model_2013.pdf [Accessed 01/10/19]
[24] Ibid
[25] Ibid

mentions; 'Our brains are biological organs by their very nature. Any disorder is in its essence a biological process.'[26]

The primary pharmacological treatments for Depression in the UK as recommended by NICE are tricyclic antidepressants (TCAs), selective serotonin re-uptake inhibitors (SSRIs), and monoamine oxidase inhibitors (MAOIs), most of which have an antagonistic effect on neurotransmitter pathways.[27] In the last decade the NHS has seen nearly double the amount of antidepressants being prescribed (from 33.7 million in 2006 to 64.7 million in 2016).[28] Whilst studies have shown that when prescribed, antidepressant compliance has improved, leading to longer term prescribing for individual patients,[29] concerns have been raised not only around the number of antidepressants prescribed, but also the trend seen in the strength of the same antidepressant prescribed increasing over the last decade.[30] Concerns have been raised that antidepressants are being over-

[26] Losing the mind. (2003) Los Angeles Times. [ONLINE] Available at: https://www.latimes.com/archives/la-xpm-2003-oct-26-tm-survivors43-story.html [Accessed 01/10/19]

[27] Antidepressant drugs. (2020) NICE. [ONLINE] Available at: https://bnf.nice.org.uk/treatment-summary/antidepressant-drugs.html [Accessed 01/03/20]

[28] Antidepressants were the area with largest increase in prescription items in 2016. (2017) NHS Digital. [ONLINE] Available at: https://digital.nhs.uk/news-and-events/news-archive/2017-news-archive/antidepressants-were-the-area-with-largest-increase-in-prescription-items-in-2016 [Accessed 01/10/19]

[29] Mars, B., Heron, J., Kessler, D., Davies, N. M., Martin, R. M., Thomas, K. H., & Gunnell, D. (2017). Influences on antidepressant prescribing trends in the UK: 1995-2011. Social psychiatry and psychiatric epidemiology, 52(2), pp. 193–200.

[30] Revealed: Massive rise in antidepressant prescribing. (2019) RTE. [ONLINE] Available at: https://www.rte.ie/news/investigations-unit/2019/0218/1031271-massive-rise-antidepressant-prescribing/ [Accessed 01/03/20]

prescribed as a result of the influence of the pharmaceutical industry.[31]

The cognitive (or lack there-of) condition of Depression stems from the same pathophysiological pathway, in that cognitive impairment stems from the same defects in neural circuitry.[32] In specific, research has suggested that these neural defects cause a decrement in cognition by way of reduced motivation, attenuated attentional capacity, impaired concentration, intrusive thought and slowness.[33] Cognitive Behavioural therapy (CBT) provides a strategy to reverse these maladaptive cognitions through behaviour based problem-solving techniques.[34] It is described as 'a collaborative problem-solving process to test and challenge the validity of maladaptive cognitions and to modify maladaptive behavioural patterns.'[35] Whilst CBT is often recommended as a first line option under the NICE mild to moderate Depression treatment pathway,[36] the referral pathways from General Practice to psychological therapies are not always clear for patients. The DHSC devised a program for self-referral in 2008 known as Improving Access to Psychological Therapies (IAPT).[37] However,

---

[31] Ibid.

[32] Trivedi J. K. (2006). Cognitive deficits in psychiatric disorders: Current status. Indian journal of psychiatry, 48(1), pp. 10–20.

[33] Ibid.

[34] Hofmann, S. G., Asnaani, A., Vonk, I. J., Sawyer, A. T., & Fang, A. (2012). The Efficacy of Cognitive Behavioural Therapy: A Review of Meta-analyses. Cognitive therapy and research, 36(5), pp. 427–440.

[35] Ibid.

[36] NICE, Step 2: Recognised depression in adults – persistent subthreshold depressive symptoms or mild to moderate depression

[37] Thomas, F. Hansford, L. Ford, J. Wyatt, K. McCabe, R. & Byng, R. (2019) How accessible and acceptable are current GP referral mechanisms for IAPT for low-income patients? Lay and primary care perspectives, Journal of Mental Health, DOI: 10.1080/09638237.2019.1677876 [Accessed 03/02/20]

research has shown that the process of self-referral has in fact caused a disconnect between GP and patient and is fraught with basic barriers such as; How do I know that I can self-refer? If the first appointment is free, will the rest cost? How do I self-refer if I do not have access to the internet? And so on.[38] These barriers have been seen to have disempowered patients, thus the need for a more supportive, person-centred approach.[39]

Depression represents one of the largest and most longer-term impacting mental health condition categories.[40] In recent years the DHSC has mentioned better outcomes for individuals with mental health issues are as a result of its 2012 strategy.[41] However, when looking deeper in to the matter, the overall number of people with mental health conditions has not dropped significantly. In fact, how they cope with mental health is seemingly becoming much worse.[42] When it comes to identification and recognition of Depression the NICE guidelines currently focus on individuals that have self-referred. They state that if a practitioner is 'not competent to perform a mental health assessment, they should refer the person to a professional. If this professional is not the person's GP, inform the GP of the referral.'

[38] Ibid

[39] Ibid

[40] National Institute for Health and Care Excellence (2011). Common health problems: Identification and pathways to care.

[41] HM Government Department of Health and Social Care (2017). Preventing Suicide in England: third progress report of the cross-government outcomes strategy to save lives.

[42] National Institute for Health and Care Excellence (2009). Depression In Adults: Recognition and Management. [ONLINE] Available at https://www.nice.org.uk/guidance/cg90/resources/depression-in-adults-recognition-and-management-pdf-975742638037 [Accessed 13/12/19]

The individual would then be risk assessed and then treatment options would be provided.[43]

2.2 The Islamic perspective

Muslims across varied backgrounds and traditions are in no way a monolith, and as such studies conducted into the perceptions of Muslims in western societies around mental health show a wide variation in their respective attitudes.[44] On the one hand is the perception of mental health conditions and their clinical treatments being mutually exclusive to religious tradition, and on the other hand is the perception that both are complimentary, thus perpetuating the stigma around mental health furthermore.

Hence the relationship with mental health conditions such as Depression and the perceptions of it amongst the Muslim community has never been monolithic. Although at *prima facie* western General Practitioners are trusted and relied upon for sound advice and treatment in such matters, their lack of cultural and religious competence in understanding the plethora of perceptions of mental

---

[43] Ibid

[44] Weatherhead, S. Davies, A. (2010) Muslim views on mental health and psychotherapy: The British Psychological Society. [ONLINE] Available at https://www.researchgate.net/publication/26794589_Muslim_views_on_mental_health_and_psychotherapy. [Accessed 13/12/19]

health conditions within the Muslim community produces less than efficacious results.[45]

The former view holds that Islam provides Muslims with a code of behaviour, ethics, and social values, which helps them in tolerating and developing adaptive coping strategies to deal with stressful life events, and as such a weakness in mental health is owed solely to a weakness in faith quoting verses of the Qur'an such as:

'...And whoever relies upon Allah - then He is sufficient for him (Quran, 65:3).'[46]

The latter view however, uses its own evidences such as the Hādith of the Prophet Muhammad that 'Allah has sent down both the disease and the cure, and He has appointed a cure for every disease, so treat yourselves medically, but use nothing unlawful' to support their view that the Islamic perspective and the clinical assessment and treatment of mental health conditions go hand in hand.[47, 48]

In this milieu of subjective interpretation of scripture and the sayings of the Prophet and his companions, the Islamic world had seen some major contributions towards the study of mental health conditions

[45] Rassool, G. H. (2018) Evil Eye, Jinn Possession, and Mental Health Issues: An Islamic Perspective (Explorations in Mental Health). Oxon, UK: Routledge. pp.4
[46] Sabry, W. Vohra, A. (2013) Role of Islam in the management of Psychiatric disorders. Indian Journal of Psychiatry. [ONLINE] Available at:
https://www.ncbi.nlm.nih.gov/pmc/articles/PMC3705684/?report=printable#rcf5 [Accessed 13/12/19]
[47] Sulaymān ibn al-Ash'ath, A, D. (2008) Sunan Abu Dawud. English Translation. New York: Darussalam International publications. Volume 4, pp. 312
[48] Sabry, W. Vohra, A. (2013)

such as Depression and its treatments. Bringing together the physical aspects of mental health conditions and their medicinal remedies, as well as understanding the cognitive and spiritual aspects of the conditions polymaths such as Abu Zayd al-Balkhi (d.934) pioneered the idea of cognitive behavioural therapy well before its time.[49] Al-Balkhi's works such as *Masālih al-Abdān wa al-Anfus* (Sustenance for Body and Soul) are the first known works to discuss the physiological impact of psychosocial conditions (and visa-versa) and also the first of its kind to discuss in depth the different techniques that could form systematic desensitization therapy, and how religious cognitive approaches can help the body and soul.[50]

Al-Balkhi's works were not the only pioneering approaches to mental health in the Islamic world. Abū Bakr Muhammad ibn Zakariyyā al-Rāzī's (d. 925) *Kitāb al-Ḥāwī fī al-ṭibb* was also a pioneering piece of work disseminated into 23 volumes and printed repeatedly in the western world around the fifteenth and sixteenth centuries.[51] Al-Razi was acutely aware of the interlinking of mental health conditions with the cognitive and physiological, and stated that 'the state of the body is linked to the state of the mind.'[52]

[49] Badri, M. (2013) Abu Zayd al-Balkhi's sustenance of the soul the cognitive behaviour therapy of a ninth century physician. Herndon, USA: the international institute of islamic thought.
[50] Ibid, pp.30-33
[51] Tibi S. (2006). Al-Razi and Islamic medicine in the 9th century. Journal of the Royal Society of Medicine, 99(4), 206–207. [ONLINE] Available at: https://doi.org/10.1258/jrsm.99.4.206 [Accessed 01/10/19]
[52] Ibid

2.3 Mental health stigma

The early and exponential expansion of the Islamic world brought with it a lot of economic prosperity. Not only was there unprecedented importation of agricultural goods into the Mediterranean, as well as greater access to a new South Asia market, the Islamic world enjoyed much wealth over all of the social strata, and so in the first three to four hundred years significant emphasis was placed on the proliferation of knowledge.[53]

The first recognised mental health institution in Europe was set up around the thirteenth century in London, five centuries after the establishment of the first psychiatric hospital in Baghdad (705 CE).[54] Yet despite the Muslim worlds advancements in the field of psychiatry, mental health stigma is profound in the Muslim community.[55] Cultural differences can have significant implications with respect to mental health stigma, and studies such as the Marrow and Luhrmann study (2012) show that contrasting perceptions of mental health, shame, honour, moral responsibility, access to mental health services are indeed extremely different with developing countries such as India, contrasted with the United States.[56]

---

[53] Gutas, D. (1997) Greek thought, Arabic culture. London, UK: Taylor and Francis group. pp. 12-13

[54] Tzeferakos, G.A., Douzenis, A.I. (2017) Islam, mental health and law: a general overview. Ann Gen Psychiatry Volume 16, p.28. [ONLINE] Available at: https://doi.org/10.1186/s12991-017-0150-6 Accessed [12/02/20]

[55] Ciftci, A. Jones, N. Corrigan, P. (2012) Journal of Muslim Mental health: Mental health stigma in the Muslim community. Michigan, USA: Michigan Publishing, Volume 7, Issue 1, pp. 17-31.

[56] Marrow, J., & Luhrmann, T. M. (2012). The zone of social abandonment in cultural geography: On the street in the United States, inside the family in India. Culture,

When examining the relationship between Muslims and mental health stigma, the discussion requires some contextual narrative. Islamic clinicians and theologians alike have always understood illness to be a condition linked to the divine. The Prophet Muhammad is reported to have said:

'No Muslim is afflicted with harm because of sickness or some other inconvenience, but that Allah will remove his sins for him as a tree sheds its leaves.'[57]

As such any illness is therefore regarded as God decreed (Qadr), and a test from God.[58] Studies have suggested that an individual's perception of Qadr and acceptance of God's divine plan have led to greater optimism with respect to healing, in turn leading to more positive outcomes.[59]

Yet despite the theological understanding of the nature of illness itself being relatively universal, many people within the Muslim community reject the notion of the physiological, cognitive or behavioural foundations of mental health conditions, and regard them as cases of Jinn (evil spirits) possession, or ones lack of spiritual connection with

medicine and psychiatry, 1-21.

[57] Bukhāri, M. I. I. (1997). Sahih Al-Bukhari: English Translation. Riyadh, Saudi Arabia: Darussalam publishers.
Hādith 5660.

[58] Ciftci, A. Jones, N. Corrigan, P. (2012), pp.23

[59] Nabolsi, M. M., & Carson, A. M. (2011) Spirituality, illness, and personal responsibility: The experience of Jordanian Muslim men with coronary artery disease. Scandinavian Journal of Caring Sciences, 25, pp.716-724.

the divine.[60] Even those with a positive attitude towards mental health conditions were found to be reluctant in discussing the issue due to social stigma.[61] The issue of social stigma therefore requires managing within the community itself, and Imams can add great value in breaking down barriers.

Jinn possession

Our study need not concern itself with the different theological understandings of the authenticity or nature of Jinn possession, though there are numerous verses in the Qur'an and Hādith that explain the nature of Jinn.[62] Our first research question was around whether Imams were able to identify symptoms of Depression so they can then support their congregants better (if they have the necessary training) or can refer appropriately. Where Jinn possession, evil eye and such alike are concerned in respect of Depression our literature review has shown Depression in particular has been regarded as possibly a cognitive, physiological and/or spiritual condition by the orthodoxy. Yet it still forms part of the thought process of perceived causation for mental health problems experienced by individuals within the Muslim community.[63] A study looking in to peoples beliefs

---

[60] Al-Adawi, S., Dorvlo, A. S., Al-Ismaily, S. S., & et al. (2002) Perception of and attitude towards mental illness in Oman. The International Journal of Social Psychiatry, Volume 48, pp.305-317.

[61] Aloud, N., & Rathur, A. (2009) Factors affecting attitudes towards seeking and using formal mental health and psychological services among Arab Muslim populations. Journal of Muslim Mental Health, 4, 79-103. [ONLINE] Available at: http://dx.doi.org/10.1080/15564900802487675 Accessed [03/02/20]

[62] Al Ashqar, Umar S. (2003) The World of the Jinn and Devils in the Light of the Qur'an and Sunnah. UK: International Islamic Publishing House. pp.10-12

[63] Lim, A., Hoek, H. W., Ghane, S., Deen, M., & Blom, J. D. (2018) The Attribution of Mental Health Problems to Jinn: An Explorative Study in a Transcultural Psychiatric

around Jinn possession (on behalf of the Royal College of Psychiatrists) in Leicester and Dhaka showed that 52% of respondents (58 out of 111) in Leicester believed that mental health issues were caused by Jinn possession (as opposed to 44% in Dhaka).[64] So, it could be assumed that the 52% of respondents that view mental health conditions as a form of Jinn possession, could also come with some cultural biases. The issue of cultural bias in relation to Jinn possession has been explored in various studies.[65] Most recently a similar study conducted in Netherlands showed that only 17% of Muslims interviewed in the Netherlands believed mental health conditions to be caused by Jinn possession.[66] In the UK people tend not to live in isolation from their own community of people, and the close links with the countries of origin foster continuity of beliefs between the community in the UK, and the community abroad (the country of origin). Being part of a modern secular country therefore does not necessarily transform beliefs about illness causation.[67]

The Study on behalf of The Royal College of Psychiatrists recommended the following:

Outpatient Clinic. *Frontiers in psychiatry*, *9*, 89. [ONLINE] Available at: https://doi.org/10.3389/fpsyt.2018.00089 Accessed [20/08/20]

[64] Khalifa, N, Hardie, T, Mullick. (2012) Jinn and Psychiatry: Comparison of Beliefs among Muslims in Dhaka and Leicester. Publications Archive: Royal College of Psychiatrists' Spirituality and Psychiatry Special Interest Group, [ONLINE] Available at: http://www.rcpsych.ac.uk/workinpsychiatry/specialinterestgroups/spirituality/publicationsarchive.aspxk). [Accessed 20/08/20]

[65] Lim, A., Hoek, H. W., Ghane, S., Deen, M., & Blom, J. D. (2018)

[66] Ibid

[67] Ibid

'Practitioners need to be mindful that beliefs about Jinn and resorting to supernatural explanations at time of distress are an easily identifiable part of the Islamic culture. Clinicians need to be prepared to enlist the help of religious figures if necessary, although the underlying mental disorders should be treated using conventional psychiatric methods.'

Therefore, Imams can play a vital role in supporting clinicians by not only guiding people spiritually but by allaying some of the cultural biases these congregants would have. This would in turn provide better patient outcomes for Practitioners. This however would mean a proper referral process visa-versa, as well as training and support for Imams.

2.4 Imams

Whilst the etymology of the word Imam has its foundations from the root Amma meaning to head for, or to lead,[68] broadly the term refers an individual that has received a level of knowledge and piety that renders them an example and leader to others.[69] The epistemological foundations of the word is directly derived from the Qur'an as God mentions in respect of his Prophets as Imams to their people.[70] Our study aims to look in particular at mosque-based Imams. The

---

[68] Al-Hilli, A. (1928) Al-Bābu al-hadi 'ashar. English translation by W. M. Miller. London, UK: Royal Asiatic Society, pp. 392.

[69] At-Tabari, I.J. (2000) Jami' al-Bayan fi Ta'wil al-Qur'an. Translated by Michael Fishbein. Los Angeles, USA: State University of New York Press, pp. 18.

[70] Qur'an 25:74, Qur'an 46:12, Qur'an 2:124

Department for Communities and Local Government have defined the role of the mosque-based Imam as an individual that 'leads the congregational prayers and gives the Friday khutbah (sermon); leads other major events at the mosque; conducts ceremonies in relation to births, marriages and deaths; provides advice on matters of Fiqh (Islamic jurisprudence); guides spirituality; teaches the young how to read the Qur'an and how to perform the five daily prayers and discharges other religious duties; and may supervise a deputy or assistant imam.'[71]

Thus, when it comes to the role of Imams many see a spiritual element to the condition of Depression, as well as a clinical one.[72] And so, the counselling and treatment offered through an Imam is likely to be very different to that of clinical practitioners, and may even differ from Imam to Imam. This then leads to a disjointed level of care for an individual that may get one answer from a GP, and a different response from the Imam.

In the literature review Imams have certainly been identified as a group that can have a clear impact on their community, in their roles as spiritual guides as well as community leaders, mediators,

[71] Communities and Local Government. (2010) The training and development of Muslim Faith Leaders. [ONLINE] Available at:
https://assets.publishing.service.gov.uk/government/uploads/system/uploads/attachm ent_data/file/6155/1734121.pdf, pp. 30, [Accessed 01/10/2019]
[72] Ali, M, O. Milstein. G. (2012) Journal of Muslim Mental health: Mental Illness Recognition and Referral Practices Among Imams in the United States. Michigan, USA: Michigan Publishing, Volume 6, Issue 2, pp. 3-13.

counsellors and advisors.[73] Surveys of public belief about Professionals have shown that the public appreciates non-conventional sources for help and support with mental health conditions.[74] Another finding which is striking is that counsellors are more likely than psychologists to be seen as potentially helpful for a range of mental disorders, despite psychologists being nationally registered professionals, whereas councillors can be unregulated.[75] This therefore gives scope to the training and nurturing of Imams to be able to support, counsel and guide those with Depression, and be seen in a positive light.

2.5 Other research in this area

Research has been conducted to combine both approaches to care (spiritual and clinical), and a subsequent recommendation has been set out to create 'self-help' Islamic prayers in addition to clinical treatment options.[76] Whilst this is a step in the right direction in allowing those that suffer with mental health conditions to express their religious values through positive religious coping mechanisms, it doesn't address the issues surrounding early recognition, and nor does it address protocol for referral. Self-help books also put the entire ownness on the individual to be solely in charge of their own health,

---

[73] Rahman, S. Ahmed, S. Khan, S. (2006) Voices from the minarets: MCB study of UK imams and mosques.

[74] Jorm, A. (2011) Mental Health Literacy: Empowering the Community to Take Action for Better Mental Health.

[75] Ibid.

[76] Mir, G. (2014). Adapted behavioural activation for the treatment of depression in Muslims. [ONLINE] Available at: http://medhealth.leeds.ac.uk/info/615/research/327/addressing_depression_in_musli m_communitis [Accessed 13/12/19]

and accountable for it. Similarly e-learning and online modules that do similar have been proven to be no more effective than a normal GP appointment.

The closest research in this area has been the study by Ali and Milstein (2012) in the Journal of Muslim Mental health titled Mental Illness Recognition and Referral Practices Among Imams in the United States.[77] The paper was largely quantitative, and focussed around three main areas:

1. Could Imams recognise the severity of a mental health problem?
2. Would Imams be willing to refer a person with symptoms of a serious mental disorder to a clinician?
3. Do age, consultation experience, or counselling training correlate with collaboration between Imams and mental health professionals?[78]

Some clear outcomes were also presented in the paper, namely:

i.   Healthcare planners need to recognise that Imams can recognise serious mental health problems.
ii.   Imams are an important source for referrals and influence on the attitudes towards mental health.

---

[77] Ali, M, O. Milstein, G. (2012) Mental Illness Recognition and Referral Practices Among Imams in the USA

[78] Ibid

iii.   Greater collaboration with Imams may lead to Muslim
       communities being more likely to utilise community
       resources and clinicians.[79]

However, there were some key issues with the study. The study was
conducted in the USA, which serves different demographics to that in
the city of Leicester. Secondly (a major failing perhaps) the research
focussed on mental health in general. We know that mental health
conditions are of various types, and different epistemologies. You
therefore cannot have a one size fits all approach to mental health.
The study also presented a vignette and asked whether the Imam
would class it as a mental health condition. Mental health conditions,
and especially Depression can precipitate much deeper signs and
symptoms that would not be as clear as this scenario has presented.
So the Ali, Milstein study gives a good starting point to present a
similar study in the UK with some key differences:

-   A qualitative study is needed for an in-depth analysis of the
    perceptions of Imams.
-   Our study focuses on Depression rather than mental health in
    general.
-   How can we take the Ali, Milstein study further? If indeed the
    Ali, Milstein study shows that cross-sector collaboration is
    needed, is there an appetite for this with Imams? And if so,
    what would this look like?

---

[79] Ibid

3. Methodology

The research problem to discussed was: can Imams form part of a cross-sector referral process to support the mental health needs of their populations, in specific in relation to Depression?

Therefore, it follows that my approach to this research is qualitative. This will allow me to engage in dialogue with the participants and understand their different perceptions in relation to the two key themes being considered in this study, namely;

1. Are Imams aware of signs and symptoms of Depression?

2. Can a combined cross-sector approach to care be formulated whereby Imams also play a role in the mental wellbeing of individuals alongside other professionals?

(refer back to introduction)

3.1 Study design

The epistemological landscape of qualitative data research can be varied and convoluted. Thus, the approach to this work stems from the hermeneutical foundations laid out by Anthony Giddens in his approach to social scientific study. It is acknowledged that the natural sciences present an empiricism that is clear and logical, whilst social science has a 'more complex relationship with its subject matter, in that the claims of social science have to be defended vis-à-vis the agents who's activities they claim to explain.'[80] Giddens proposes a double hermeneutic methodology in which social scientific discourse penetrates the natural sciences, and in doing so changes the model of research from an instrumental or technical one, to one that is dialogical and collaborative.[81]

This approach combined with an interpretivist philosophy forms the fundamental part of this research. Geoff Walsham describes interpretive research as:

'Interpretive methods of research start from the position that our knowledge of reality, including the domain of human action, is a social construction by human actors and that this applies equally to researchers.'[82]

As such the researcher acts as a social actor and appreciates the differences between people's opinions, searching for a deeper understanding into the issue in question.[83] It therefore follows that the research will follow an exploratory case study design methodology. Case study research involves understanding the important contextual conditions pertinent to the case (Depression –

---

[80] Tucker, K. (1998) Anthony Giddens and modern social theory. California, USA: Sage publications, pp.59.

[81] Tucker, K. pp. 61

[82] Walsham, G. (1995) The Emergence of Interpretivism in IS Research. Information Systems Research, 6(4), 376-394. [ONLINE] Available at: www.jstor.org/stable/23010981 [Accessed 01/10/2019]

[83] Saunders, M., Lewis, P. & Thornhill, A. (2012) Research Methods for Business Students. 6th edition. UK: Pearson Education Limited

and the scope for referral from/to Imams),[84] and an exploratory case study research design is needed here because the 'case' which we are evaluating has no clear single set of outcomes.[85]

3.2 Limitations of qualitative semi-structured research

Qualitative research can have many limitations. We are dealing often with a large amount of often deep and thought-provoking conversation. The analysis and conclusions need to be carefully hedged, because the information gained may not be easily quantifiable, or generalisable. Another limitation with qualitative data, is that in this case we are dealing with perceptions. Perceptions of human beings are changeable, but at the same time, they can as Giddens puts it 'have the persuasive power to modify people's knowledge about their social world, so that they can change their behaviour accordingly.[86] Conversely having done an extensive literature review, the interviewer too has to be careful not to allow findings and research to influence the interviewees thoughts and conclusions. Yin (2003) states that 'too many times a case study researcher has been sloppy, has not followed systematic process and has allowed equivocal evidence to influence the direction of the findings and conclusions.'[87]

---

[84] Yin, R. K. (2003) Case study research: Design and methods, 3rd edition. California, USA: Sage publications, pp.16
[85] Ibid.
[86] Tucker, K. pp.61
[87] Yin, R. K. (2003) pp. 20

The interviewer also has to consider that the semi structured interview style is less likely encompass a large amount of interviewees, hence there is a delicate balance between having a large enough sample to yield a substantive outcome and have the time, resources and labour to be able to analyse, extract and derive substantial outcomes from the data.[88] Yet the researcher must be very careful to hedge any conclusions or generalizations based on such a research design very carefully. A common concern for a study of such nature is that the information provided is not always empirical, and whilst experiments can be generalised, it is not as easy to generalise qualitative case study based data.[89] I would however disagree with that hypothesis. Generalisations based on data from experiments are repeated, often under different conditions. Such an approach can also be taken with qualitative case study data. The theoretical propositions can be used to expand current theories, add to the multiplicity of work, or provide different conditions for the case study entity (Depression in our case).

Yin (2003) states that case study research can 'potentially take too long and that they can result in massive unreadable documents.'[90] Thus the research methodology has to be about striking a balance between:

---

[88] Newcomer, K. Hatry, H. Wholey, J. (2015) Handbook of practical program evaluation. 4th edition. Jersey, USA: Joh Wiley & Sons inc. pp 27.
[89] Yin, R. K. (2003) pp. 20
[90] Ibid, pp. 21

- How much do we delve into the topic (scope)?
- Time constraints
- Resources

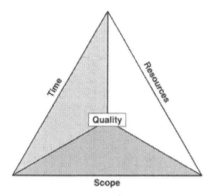

Figure 3.1

Time, Resources, and Scope triangle

Inevitably, an increase in one area would mean compromising another.[91] The semi structured interview process will allow the interviewer to home in with closed questions if need be, to ensure that all the necessary information is gained in a time bound manner.

Further Limitations

A major limitation of the study may seem as it is male focused. Nearly all Imams in the UK are male, and the likelihood is that their congregation is mostly male. Therefore, chances are that any interaction that Imams may have had with individuals regarding their Depression would have been male. Though data analysis in Leicester

[91] Given, L. (editor) (2008) The Sage encyclopaedia of qualitative research methods. Volume 2. California, USA: Sage publications, pp.810

shows that cases of suicide in Leicester in males year on year is always greater than women (in the last three years, over 13 males committed suicide per 100,000 population, compared to just under 5 per 100,000 population for women) Depression affects every type of Demography, and hence if female participation in this study is minimal, this is indeed a limitation. Any future study would therefore need to possibly take in to consideration the lack of spiritual support provided to females, that men are exposed to at mosques.

Secondly, this study does not differentiate economic, and ethnic disparities. Leicester has a high population of ethnic minorities, and hence this may skew the results depending on their perceptions. A research proposal on ethnic minorities and their view on Depression in Leicester may be considered here. This could supplement out study, ensure that the nature of the demography is understood better.

Thirdly, another limitation of the study is that once the formula (see below) has been used to identify the number of Imams to interview within a domination, I will be contacting the Imams directly due to the limitation in time. This means that those Imams that are harder to access (no email accounts, or telephone numbers publicly available) would potentially miss the opportunity to participate. Hence, it will not be a totally random list. The reasons for this are that I wish to engage as many Imams as possible, and not have a sample size smaller than 10. Nevertheless, the denominations will be represented respective to the number of mosques they have in Leicester. Another downside of this is that the number of mosques does not necessarily represent the number of people that follow that mosque, so that may also have to be considered. You could have one Imam that has a very small congregation, hence fewer potential cases of Depression and another Imam with a lot more cases. However, despite an Imam having a smaller congregation (and less potential cases of congregants with Depressive symptoms) it does not automatically follow that the Imam therefore does not recognise the signs and symptoms of Depression.

Due to finance, time and budget, I have selected only the city of Leicester. Whilst the results may shed light on to the perceptions of Imams in Leicester this may only act as a *pilot* view of the opinions of Imams across the country that may be exposed to different demographics, social and cultural norms.

3.3 Sampling and rationale

In qualitative research of this kind consideration has to be given to the appropriateness of interviewees chosen and access to them. The literature review showed that Imams are very much regarded as community leaders and support congregants with their spiritual and emotional needs. Whilst Ulamā (and this includes Mufti's) could have been chosen, Imams in general are in more regular conversation with their congregants, and as a result would have a potentially greater experience of counselling with respect to Depression.[92] The study recognises that in asking specifically Imams this would leave out females (Aalima's) who would potentially be just as suitably qualified. This is a key limitation of the study. In recognising this issue, it will also form part of a theme in the semi-structured interview and can be addressed as part a separate study to add to the breadth of what has already been done in this area.

The next part of the process was to identify the mosques and Imams to send an invite for participation in the study to (Appendix A). According to muslimsinbritain.org there are 73 mosques in Leicester.[93] The study focussed on interviewing up to 15 Imams in Leicester from various communities with an aim to have at least a minimum sample size of 10. This number was chosen due to the nature of qualitative data research, and the amount of work that needs to go into interview preparation, the interview itself, and the subsequent analysis of data.

The Muslim Council of Britain has recognised the need to unify the various denominations of Islam,[94] and as such the research was open to interviewing all denominations that refer to themselves as Muslim. The denominational breakdown was recognised as Sunni and Shi'a, as

---

[92] Ulamā is the plural form of the word Aalim referring to someone who has completed studies on Islamic education at the tertiary level. A Mufti would have completed a specialisation course (Iftā) in a specific area of Islamic jurisprudence (Fiqh).

[93] Muslims in Britain (2018). Mosques in Leicestershire. [ONLINE] Available at:

https://mosques.muslimsinbritain.org/maps.php#/town/Leicester [Accessed 14/12/19]

[94] MCB (2015). Terrorists cannot divide us. [ONLINE] Available at:

https://mcb.org.uk/general/unity-home-meeting-160115/ [Accessed 14/12/19]

the various inter-denominational groups within them, would identify as either of the two.

According to the mosque representation the following formula was used based on mosque demographics in Leicester:

(Number of mosques of denomination in Leicester / 73) x 15 = x (rounded up)

So, there are 3 Shia mosques - I will be interviewing (3/73) x15 = 0.61 = 1 Shia Imam.

Breakdown of potential participants:

Sunni (self-identified)	14
Shi'a (self-identified)	1

Due to the nature of the research, participants were chosen by contacting them directly. Initial contact was be made over the telephone by inviting the Imams to participate in the study. They were then sent an information letter along with a consent form to sign (Appendix A and Appendix B).

The criteria for selection were be based on:
- Participants must be within the remit of 14 Sunni, and 1 Shi'a (as above)
- The mosque must be open for five daily prayers (so that the researcher is confident in knowing that the Imam has contact time with congregants)

- The mosque must have recognised Imam(s) – known by the community to be the Imam(s) of the mosque.

Imams were then contacted accordingly. It is recognised that a limitation of the study is that there could still be a subjective bias, as the researcher is still *picking* his subjects of study. However, as the researcher has no preconceived hypothesis on what type of responses, he would get to the questions asked in this study, the level of subjective bias is somewhat minimised. It was important to pick the participants to get quality data as the sample size was up to 15. It was also recognised that the mosques having a facility available for females to pray is not part of the criteria. As previously discussed, the importance of recognising the counselling needs of the female of population as well as the that of the male population with respect to Depression means that this criterion remains open to recognise the presence/lack of provision of services for females in mosques.

The semi structured interview started with a series of closed questions to ensure that demographic data is obtained, as some of the questions would help address key issues raised in the data analysis (see Appendix C).

Below explains the interview structure with timings:

TASK	TIME
Introduction to topic Acknowledgment of receipt of consent and participant understand purpose of study	3 minutes
Initial closed questions	7 minutes
Open questions in depth	25 minutes
TOTAL TIME	35 minutes

Figure 3.2

Interview timings

The semi-structured interviews were recorded on a secure audio recording facility on my laptop. Each audio recording was given a pseudonym and stored in password protected file. Permission was sought for this (Appendix B). Recording allowed me to focus on the participants answers and continue the flow of the conversation. The information from the recordings was then transcribed by myself to make data extraction easier. The transcription was done on MS Word. All of the transcribed data was then stored on a password protected file on my laptop, which also requires a password to access it.

3.4 Rationale for closed and open question in semi-structured interview questions

The closed questions aimed to bring into account variables such as age, experience, previous training, length of time in UK (if not born), etc.... This data was quantitative and would be used to influence our understanding by showing us how truly reflective our sample is. It will also help us analyse our Qualitative data better, as it will give us an understanding of whether age, experience, or any other variables impact people's perceptions.

Closed questions do come with limitations. As the structure of closed questioning is largely quantitative it does not allow the interviewee to elaborate nor allow for the interviewer to prompt the respondent if they are having difficulty in answering a question. Regular prompting only increases the time (see figure 3.1) leading to having to make adjustments in other areas. There is also the potential for misunderstanding or misinterpretation, as the interview is in English, which may not be the first language of some of the respondents.

The open semi structured interview questions come from the following:

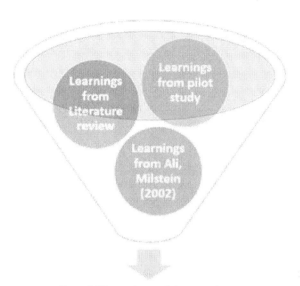

Semi Structured Interview
questions

Figure 3.3

Semi structured interview questions

The literature review allows the researcher to establish the themes around which the key questions are to be asked, and in the pilot study the researcher is able to refine the questions to generate quality responses. A similar study conducted in the USA (Ali, Milstein, 2012) can allow the researcher to take learnings from what went well and not so well. Though the Ali, Milstein study was more of a quantitative survey it enables the researcher to take some unanswered questions to another level, or even add depth to what is already there.

Though the semi structured interviews were expected to take place in person, Covid-19 has had a significant impact due to the lockdown restrictions imposed by the Department of Health and Social Care on the 23rd March 2020.[95] Whilst restrictions had eased nationally, Leicester was subject to further lockdown measures (following temporary easing of restrictions) on the 4th July 2020.[96]

As a result, all the interviews took place over the phone, and were audio recorded on the laptop (with prior permission sought as per GDPR guidelines, see Appendix B). The recorded files were stored in a secure password encrypted folder, then transcribed by me in a password protected file.

3.5 Ethical considerations

My research requires the data gathering to be in accordance with the British Educational Research Association's (BERA) guidelines,[97] as well as the ethical guidelines for Research in the Counselling Professions as recommended by NICE.[98] Some of the premises that I visit may include

---

[95] DHSC. (2020) Prime Minister's statement on coronavirus (COVID-19): 23 March 2020 [ONLINE] Available at: https://www.gov.uk/government/speeches/pm-address-to-the-nation-on-coronavirus-23-march-2020 [Accessed 01/08/20]

[96] DHSC. (2020) Meeting people from outside your household: guidance for Leicester [ONLINE] Available at:
https://www.gov.uk/government/publications/local-lockdown-guidance-for-social-distancing/meeting-people-from-outside-your-household-guidance-for-leicester [Accessed 20/08/20]

[97] BERA (2018) Ethical guidelines for educational research. [ONLINE] Available at: https://www.bera.ac.uk/researchers-resources/publications/ethical-guidelines-for-educational-research-2018 [Accessed 14/12/19]

[98] BACP. (2018) Ethical Guidelines for Research in the Counselling Professions. [ONLINE] Available at: https://www.bacp.co.uk/media/3908/bacp-ethical-guidelines-for-research-counselling-professions.pdf [Accessed 14/12/19]

an educational institute for under 16s. As a result, I have already got an Enhanced Disclosure and Barring Service (DBS) clearance from 2019 from my current Employer, Lexon Pharmaceuticals Ltd. This however was not needed as due to Covid-19 restrictions all contact was made remotely.

Ethical approval was gained from the Markfield Institutes Research Ethics Committee to conduct the research and an ethical approval form was submitted to Dr Ataullah Siddiqui. The research was allowed to proceed with approval on the Friday 15th May 2020.

Consent

Following the Introduction of the General Data Protection Regulation (GDPR) of 2018, participants were held to strict confidentiality and were also told about how their data will be managed. The GDPR will always allow participants to have the right to be informed; the right to have access to their data if they require, the right to rectification, the right to erasure, and the right to object if they so wish.[99] All participants were asked to clarify whether they understood the purpose of study and how long their data would be stored (Appendix B).

Transparency

Prior to participation Imams were sent an invite letter be available for interview (Appendix A). This was sent in the post, though initial

[99] Information Commissioner's office (2020) Individual rights. [ONLINE] Available at: https://ico.org.uk/for-organisations/guide-to-data-protection/guide-to-the-general-data-protection-regulation-gdpr/individual-rights/ [Accessed 01/08/20]

contact was made over the phone to illicit a better response rate.
telephone numbers were gained from what is already available
publicly online, and where the telephone number was not available
emails were sent to invite the Imam to participate in the research (see
figure 3.4).

The letter stated the purpose of the study, and the possible outcomes.
It also contained a consent form which explained confidentiality, and
that the participation of the Imams is entirely voluntary.
Should an Imam refuse participation, using the method above,
another Imam from the same denomination would be chosen. In the
course of the research and analysis, participants were given a name
reference (pseudonym) rather than their actual name. This meant that
although their views were heard, the real names of the Imams that
stated those views will not be identifiable.

Figure 3.4

Flowchart of how contact was made with Imams.

Pilot study

Prior to the interview stage, two Imams were interviewed as part of a pilot study, and they will not be included as part of the research data. This pilot will allow considerations for any adjustments needed in the questionnaires, the semis-structured interviews, or the other documents. This could mean potentially adjusting my style of interviewing, or even the wording of the documents.

Following the research conducted in USA (Ali, Milstein 2012) a key issue that came out of the study was that they were left with research that mentioned that some Imams had certain perceptions about certain things, but the study could not get clear outcomes from the knowledge gained.[100] No tangible recommendations could be made to allow for further study into possible referral mechanisms to and from Imams by/to other professionals. This requires further exploration with the individual Imams, hence why semi-structured interviews were be used.

The overall aim is to take the Ali, Milstein study further and develop a framework from which a combined approach to care for individuals within the Muslim community can be devised. Whilst the NHS is keen on faith leaders coming on board, it has not devised a method in to *how*. Through understanding the perceptions of Imams (as leaders within the community) their expertise can be utilised to develop a framework and better help those that are suffering with mental health issues such as Depression.

3.5 Methods of analysis

As the initial questions were quantitative, data was analysed through MS Excel, and each participant was coded with a pseudonym. Results were then aggregated and grouped together to provide a more meaningful analysis where required. It was not necessary to establish trends within the quantitative data itself, as the goal was to provide demographics, and supplementation to the qualitative data analysis. If

---

[100] Ali, M, O. Milstein, G. (2012)

therefore the purpose of quantitative data analysis was as stated above, I had to be careful to resist the urge to look for trends within the quantitative data itself, as this would take away from the purpose of the research and the key questions being asked.

Qualitative data analysis

The transcribed recording was an extremely large dataset and as a result the best way to make sense of this type of data was to codify it. This would allow me to understand where the key themes were emerging within the dataset. Codification of data was done by highlighting the key codes in a specific colour, such as green being the code for an Imam discussing possible causes for depressive symptoms below:

'...another issue is homesickness in immigrants. They are still homesick after 3 or 4 years here because they do not have money, nor a spouse, and are away from home..'
CODE = IDENTIFY DEPRESSIVE SYMPTOMS

Here the code used is IDENTIFY DEPRESSIVE SYMPTOMS and may come up many times during a single excerpt. The coding here is subjective, and whilst the statement above has been coded in a specific way by me, another researcher may look at it differently. However, even empirical research can have subject interpretations, and this issue is not unique to qualitative data analysis.[101] In order to

---

[101] Saldana, J. (2013) The coding manual for qualitative researchers. Los Angeles, USA: SAGE Publications. pp. 6

summarise data you may break down information that perhaps could benefit from not being coded, and can stand on its own.[102] This has been taken account of in the analysis. Another issue with coding is that it is a form of categorisation, so when faced with two opposing views on the same issue they may be categorised under the same code, though this would need be carefully hedged in the analysis.

Lofland, Snow, Anderson, & Lofland (2009), have noted that in order to study social life we must firstly identify *how* social life is organised in units and what aspects of these units can form possible study topics: [103] Thus Lofland et al (2009) have put these aspects of study in three key areas:
-   cognitive aspects or meanings (e.g., ideologies, rules, self-concepts, identities);
-   Emotional aspects or feelings (e.g., sympathy in health care, road rage, workplace satisfaction);
-   Hierarchical aspects or inequalities (e.g., racial inequality, battered women, high school cliques) [104]

These key aspects alongside Lofland et al's (2009) insight into social organisation form my methodological approach towards coding. So whilst there may be subjective interpretation of phrases, sentences, or paragraphs the coding of these datasets is process driven. Magnitude coding is the primary way in which codes are analysed in the study.

---

[102] Saldana, J. (2013), pp. 4
[103] Lofland, J. (2009). Analysing social settings: a guide to qualitative observation and analysis. California, USA: Wadsworth, pp. 13-15
[104] Ibid, pp.14

Magnitude coding allows us to identify the number of times a particular theme or code appears in a text, which may (in example) help assess the participants relative subject knowledge. However, there are some themes where magnitude coding is not appropriate. Namey et al (2008) note that in such instances, it is suggested to determine 'frequencies on the basis of the number of individual participants who mention a particular theme, rather than the total number of time a theme appears in a text...'[105] And so due to the nature of data to be analysed both magnitude as well as structural coding will form part of the analysis.

4.   Analysis and discussion

The analysis of results is based on the interviews conducted. Initially 15 Imams were contacted by phone, email, and post (see figure 3.4). In total 12 respondents agreed to participate in the study, whilst 3 were uncontactable. All 12 respondents had completed the consent forms and the interviews. All the respondent's self-identified as Sunni Muslim. Whilst two Shi'a mosques were approached (one was contacted initially, and when there was no response a second was also contacted) though none responded. It is recognised that the study therefore (by elimination) is based on Imams at Sunni (self-identified) mosques in Leicester, which may also be reflection on the denominational make-up of their congregants.

---

[105] Namey, Emily & Guest, Greg & Thairu, Lucy. (2008). Data reduction techniques for large qualitative data sets. California, USA: Sage publications. pp.143

Below is some of the quantitative data at a glance:

Questionnaires at a glance	Number of respondents					Mean
Age group	below 25	25 - 39	40 – 60	60+		40-60 years
	1	2	6	3		
Years of experience as an Imam	Less than 5 years	5 to 10 years	10 to 20 years	20 years plus		10-20 years
	2	1	4	5		
How long have you been in this country?	Born here	5 to 10 years	10 to 20 years	20 years plus		20 years plus (including born here)
	3	0	4	5		
Was your Islamic education in this country?	Yes	No	In part			Mostly Abroad
	3	6	3			
Number of vocational courses studied in addition to Islamic education	none	1 course	2 courses	3 courses	4+ courses	None
	8	1	2	1	0	
How much of your time each week is dedicated to meeting the counselling needs of your community?	zero hours	1 - 3 hours	4-6 hours	6-9 hours	9 hours +	9 hours +
	0	2	0	2	8	
How many hours a week do you work on average?	Less than 10	10 – 20	20 – 30	30 +		30+ hours
	0	0	1	11		

Figure 4.1

Quantitative data analysis

The data shows that on average the Imams in Leicester are established (mean of 10-20 years as Imam) with over 10 years of experience in their roles. The Imams interviewed on average had been in their respective communities within Leicester for over 20 years. This is in line with census data (Office for national statistics, ONS) which shows that in 2001 the city of Leicester had an 11% Muslim population, and with the 2011 census showing a 19% Muslim population.[106] At the time of the 2011 census 66 per cent of the city's usual resident population were born in the UK, and this ties in similarly with the quantitative data with respect to how long Imams have been in this country, or whether they were born here.[107] On that basis a reasonable deduction to make would be that the Imams are well versed with their demographics, and the social and spiritual needs of their communities as they themselves have (on average) been within their communities for 20 years plus.

Studying abroad

More than half the Imams interviewed stated that they had completed part if not all of their Islamic education abroad. This could be due to some of the Imams being non-UK born, or also perhaps wilfully choosing to study abroad due to the nature of Islamic education being provided abroad. Never the less, think tanks such as The Runnymede trust (the UK's leading independent race equality think tank) have mentioned this as a barrier to the Imams' effective counselling or

---

[106] Leicester city council. (2012) Census report. [ONLINE] Available at: https://www.leicester.gov.uk/media/177367/2011-census-findings-diversity-and-migration.pdf [Accessed 01/08/20]
[107] Ibid

understanding of the needs of the congregants. In their report on the challenge of Islamophobia in the UK the authors state 'The Imams and other teachers at the mosque schools mostly received their Islamic education, both secular and religious, outside Britain. There is an increasingly widespread perception in Muslim communities that Imams are not equipped by their own training to help young British Muslims cope with issues such as unemployment, racism, Islamophobia, drugs, the attraction of western youth culture, and so on.'[108] Our study establishes that the Leicester demographic of Imams as a *mean* have studied mostly or partly abroad, and on average there is no additional uptake on vocational courses in the majority; whilst this does not however directly correlate to the perception of them not being equipped to deal with modern day issues that the youth face, it shows that since the Runnymede report of 1997 there is little change in the demographic data in relation to the Imams.

However, is it conceivable that Islamic education abroad could mean that Imam's would be ill equipped to deal with the issues of their congregants closer to home? The late Dr Zaki Badawi (founder of the Muslim College, London) stated that 'Muslim communities in the West have come to rely for religious leadership on Imams and scholars whose training is mainly rooted in the cultural and educational environment of their countries of origin. This training is not always sufficient to deal with the cultural environment of modern Western Europe and the United States, nor with problems arising from interaction with Western societies.' It seems therefore that training

---

[108] The Runnnymede trust. (1997) Islamophobia: A challenge for us all. [ONLINE] Available at: https://www.runnymedetrust.org/companies/17/74/Islamophobia-A-Challenge-for-Us-All.html [Accessed 01/08/20]

abroad does not provide Imams with the necessary knowledge of secular liberal democracies, their constructs, their ethics, their challenges and so Imams would need some form of further training to deal with those challenges.[109]

Key themes have emerged in the qualitative data that has come through which shed some light in to the nature of counselling, as well it's suitability, and training needs for Imams. Nearly all of the Imams stated that they worked over 30 hours per week, and that on average 9 + hours were spend on the counselling needs of their congregants. The data shows that this represents a significant chunk of the Imams working time (on average 30% of the Imams working time).

At this point it is therefore evident that with Imams spending on average around 9 plus hours a week on counselling individual congregants, congregants *do* confide in Imams. What this looks like and how or if it could be made better is the subject of the qualitative data analysis.

---

[109] Communities and Local Government. (2010) The training and development of Muslim Faith Leaders. pp. 25

Theme 1 – Identifying signs and symptoms of Depression

One of the key questions we were asking in this study was whether Imams are aware of signs and symptoms of Depression. Our literature review identified a coherent and orthodox approach to recognising what depressive symptoms would look like within these three categories (with possible overlap in each category:

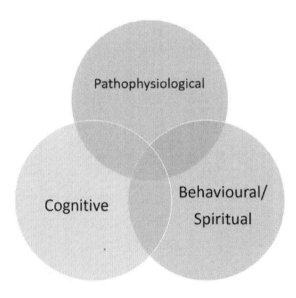

Figure 4.2

Reasons for depressive illness

The Imams were asked to identify the key signs of depressive illness within their congregants, based on the conversations that they had with their congregants. The table below allows us to contextualise the responses:

Signs of Depression as identified by Imams based on the counselling needs of their congregants	N	% of Imams that discussed the issue	How many times was the theme brought up by Imams in total?	Average mention of theme per conversation (mean)
Relationship problems b/w married couples	12	100	19	1.6
Divorce guidance	5	42	7	0.6
Looking for a spouse	1	8	2	0.2
Homesickness	1	8	1	0.1
Financial pressures	9	75	13	1.1
Cocerns about children	2	17	2	0.2
Discrimination	5	42	6	0.5
Physical abuse	1	8	1	0.1
Abused as Child	1	8	1	0.1
Suicidal thoughts	4	33	4	0.3
Drug abuse	1	8	1	0.1
Suffering from a medical issue	2	17	2	0.2
Spiritual anxiety	4	33	5	0.4
Disconnection with faith	7	58	8	0.7

N = number of Imams who identified this issue as a symptom or cause of Depression as experienced when counselling congregants

Figure 4.3

Identifying and signs and symptoms of Depression

Clinicians refer to the International Classification of Diseases (ICD-10) when recognising reasons for Depression and the severity of them.[110] When assessing for mild to moderate Depression, Clinicians look at:

- low mood, feeling sad, irritable or angry,
- having less energy to do certain things,
- losing interest or enjoyment in activities you used to enjoy,
- loss of concentration, agitated
- becoming tired more easily,
- disturbed sleep and losing your appetite,
- feeling less good about yourself (loss of self-confidence), or
- feeling guilty or worthless
- have thoughts of self-harm or suicide.[111]

The above is of course not an exhaustive list. Our Imams in addition to highlighting the issues above related this back to how the individuals *feels*.

MIL-1 stated that 'she **is feeling worthless** and says she is only in the marriage for her child.'

---

[110] Rethink mental illness (2020) Depression. [ONLINE] Available at: https://www.rethink.org/advice-and-information/about-mental-illness/learn-more-about-conditions/depression/ [Accessed 20/08/20] pp.3
[111] Ibid

SRH-1 stated that 'this man had everything, but after the break up he **now feels suicidal.**'

MAAS-1 stated that 'he always used to come in at odd times, **agitated, looking here and there**, he was clearly on drugs but was looking for a way.'

MAB-1 stated that 'questions about his faith are really **bringing him down**. He cannot sleep at night.'

Such examples show that the Imams were able to pick up on symptoms in relation to the ICD-10 and relate it back to how the reason for those depressive symptoms. This is a good platform to build on for a mutual understanding for what Depressive symptoms may look like cross-sector.

The data however does not show any reasons for Depression associated with psychotic symptoms. The ICD-10 refers to severe Depression with psychosis as 'the presence of hallucinations, delusions, psychomotor retardation, or stupor so severe that ordinary social activities are impossible; there may be danger to life from suicide, dehydration, or starvation. The hallucinations and delusions may or may not be mood-congruent.'[112] It could well be that the Imams did not recall from memory any such cases, did not have any cases at all, or did not know that psychosis could also be associated with Depression. Our literature review showed that Jinn possession and such alike were still culturally many in the Muslim community.

---

[112] ICD-10. (2010) [ONLINE] Available at https://icd.who.int/browse10/2010/en#/F32 [Accessed 20/08/20]

Could it potentially be the case that Imams would not see certain cases of psychosis as associated with Depression? Could it be thought of as Jinn possession? The issue of Jinn possession was in fact discussed by Imams in the interviews, as to whether they thought depressive illness could be caused by Jinn possession in some circumstances.

Magnitude coding was used to contextualise how many Imams were in favour of the idea of some forms of Depression being caused by Jinn possession and some not:

Can some forms of Depression be caused by Jinn Possesion?			
	In favour of	Averse to	No opinion
Number of Imams	0	9	3

Figure 4.4

Jinn possession

From the data we can derive that whilst there may be cultural biases in respect of Jinn possession amongst the community (see literature review), Imams can support to challenge these from a theological perspective, and this may useful in a cross collaborate effort with other professionals.

The responses from the Imams were very wide ranging despite all Imams negating Jinn possession for a cause of Depression. Three Imams in particular were coded with 'no opinion' due to the nature of the responses, in that they mentioned the following:

'It is difficult to say whether some types of Depression can, because were not Doctors. We are not trained on Depression.' – MIL-1

'(The) main emphasis is on purifying (the) soul, not discussing the signs of Depression. We leave that to GP.' -MAAS-1

'How can we say, we have no training in this area?' – MYK-1

These responses though coded as 'no opinion' all have a common theme, in that the Imams are more than aware of the limits of their training, and would not rush to any judgement on the state of an individuals mental health. Imams that were averse to Jinn possession being a cause of Depression could genuinely believe that Jinn possession is not part of the theological view of orthodox Islam, or perhaps that mental health issues such as Depression have a *empirical* cause to them, or perhaps may not understand the breadth of Depressive illnesses. In either case there was a vociferous response in negation of Jinn possession with respect to Depression. One Imam stated that:

'Charlatans and frauds these people are, you know, it could be schizophrenia. For example, a person has, you know, some kind of medical issue and automatically there's a Jinn, I need five hundred pounds payment and I'm going to come and sort this out. You need to do this, and ignore all medical advice, all the Islamic advice. And it's a culture thing if it's what it is.' – MNAK-1

Interestingly the Imam makes a clear the distinction between what is culture and what is Islamic. The Imam here asserts therefore that the healer is acting as a *cultural* healer rather than an Islamic one. Another Imam stated:

'Every single case has a rational medical explanation to it, every single case without exception.' – MYD-1

The results show too that the key issues for congregants as espoused by the Imams are relationship problems, financial pressures and disconnection with the faith. In order to ascertain how important these issues were to the Imams, frequency coding was used. Namey et al (2008) state that 'counting the frequency of a word or a phrase in a given data set is often a good starting point for identifying repeated ideas within a large body of text, and gives an idea of the prevalence of thematic responses across participants.[113] As such if we employ frequency coding relationship issues (and if we were also to include divorce in this too) were far and above the biggest reason for Depressive illness within their congregants, with faith related issues coming second, and financial pressures third.

---

[113] Namey, Emily & Guest, Greg & Thairu, Lucy. (2008)

Statements made by Imams in relation to Muslim women being allowed greater access in Mosques			
	In favour of	No opinion	Averse to	*Mean*
N	15	0	3	In favour of
N = number of statements made by Imams in relation to the theme			

Figure 4.5

Women and access

A theme that emerged constantly throughout the semi-structured interviews was around women and their accessibility to support from Imams. Using frequency coding each statement (sentence, or paragraph) by an Imam in relation to their perception of whether Muslim women being allowed greater access in Mosques was analysed in to three sub-categories. 100% of the Imams interviewed made positive statements in favour of greater access, and though there were three statements of disinclination they were focussed on genuine concerns for the welfare of the women involved such as:

'The husband will go to the mosque and will know that the Maulana knows about the situation and may take that out on the wife.' – MIL-1
Or
'The husband may see the wife contacted the Imam and may do horrific things.' – MIL-1

Whilst these concerns were raised the same Imams also made it categorically clear that they were in favour of 'opening-up' to the female population, as it is recognised that Muslim women are more likely to suffer from Depressive symptoms than Muslim men.[114] Whilst their challenges may be similar, Muslim women suffer from a larger proportion of anti-Muslim hate crime than their male counterparts,[115] and also have higher levels of financial distress than their male counterparts.[116]

As such, it is vital that Muslim women gain a greater level of access to support from Imams if there is to be an improvement into the disproportionality. Some key trends that were identified was that an Imam studying abroad or at home, had a negligible impact on their perception of whether Women should be granted greater access in Mosques. In fact the most vociferous comment in favour of access came from an Imam who had studied abroad fully. He stated that 'It was never like that in the Prophets time, we have regressed' and 'we have two females in our committee at the mosque and we are very proud of that.' – MAAS-1

---

[114] Eaton, N. (2015) Hijab, Religiosity, and Psychological Wellbeing of Muslim Women in the United States. Journal of Muslim Mental Health. USA: Michigan Publishing, Volume 9, issue

[115] The Runnnymede trust. (1997) Islamophobia: A challenge for us all. [ONLINE] Available at: https://www.runnymedetrust.org/companies/17/74/Islamophobia-A-Challenge-for-Us-All.html [Accessed 01/08/20]

[116] Ibid, pp.26.

Training

Data analysis shows that there are two issues that form a key barrier to cross-sector collaboration. Firstly, a lack of referral process visa-versa for those suffering with symptoms of Depression. Our analysis showed that on average over 9 hours a week are spent by Imams in supporting the counselling needs of their congregants, yet referral to other professionals is near non-existent when it comes to Depression.

How many times on average in the last 12 months have you contacted the following for any of your congregants?					
	Zero	1 to 5	6 - 10	11 - 20	20 +
General practitioner (GP)	11	1	0	0	0
Social Worker	12	0	0	0	0
Family counsellor	12	0	0	0	0
Another Imam	10	2	0	0	0
Phychiatrist/ Psychologist	10	1	1	0	0
Consultant	12	0	0	0	0
Emergency services (111)	8	4	0	0	0
Other Professional(s) (please state)	12	0	0	0	0

Figure 4.6

Contacting other professionals

We have defined referral to other professionals here as a request for specific action, assistance or guidance in relation to an individual.[117] The table above shows that very few referrals if at all took place by Imams. In total 8 out of 12 Imams had not referred at all in the last 12 months. Looking at the responses further it seems that only the transfer of care to emergency services would be classed as referrals, as in the other cases, the Imams would generally refer to another professional generically, not a specific individual case. One Imam stated:

'I have a friend who is a GP, so whenever I see him, I ask his advice on something that happened and he will give me advice. This probably happened once or twice in the last 12 months.' -MYD-1

Our study here looks into the practical aspects of referral than the theoretical. The Ali, Milstein study (2012) in the USA presented Imams with a vignette specific to Depression and asked Imams who would they refer to (if at all). It concluded that Imams would refer in such cases to professionals if presented with a similar vignette, and thus Imams were an important part of the referral process.[118] However, this does not necessary follow as in practice despite being presented with congregants with depressive symptoms (figure 4.3) very few referrals ever take place by Imams. Thus the need for a protocol of referral, which I will set out in my recommendations.

---

[117] From https://medical-dictionary.thefreedictionary.com/referral [Accessed 20/08/20]
[118] Ali, M, O. Milstein, G. (2012)

5. Conclusion and recommendations

The stigma surrounding mental health in the Muslim community is real one. Whilst discrimination, cultural views, religious interpretation and intersectionality may all have a part to play in developing that stigma,[119] these injustices leave devastating consequences for those suffering with Depression and those supporting family members with it. All sectors of society must do their bit to support those individuals, and Imams are often the first port of call for many people.

What would training look like?
Our study shows that there is an overwhelming level of recognition by Imams that in order to support the mental health needs of the communities, they would not only be open to, but in some cases 'are crying out for (mentioned by MIL in the semi structured interview)' vocational training. The late Dr Ataullah Siddiqui (may God grant him the highest of stages in paradise), commissioned by the former Department for Education and Skills supplemented this notion with the fact that a majority of Imams have received either part or all of their seminary training abroad, a greater emphasis was needed in meeting the needs of a western society with western problems. Dr Ataullah Siddiqui made some key points around the educational needs of those going through seminary training; namely:

---

[119] Ali OM, Milstein G, Marzuk P.M. (2005) The Imam's role in meeting the counselling needs of Muslim communities in the United States. [ONLINE] Available at: doi:10.1176/appi.ps.56.2.202 [Accessed 20/08/20]

- A major shift of the focus of Islamic Studies from an Arab and Middle Eastern perspective to that of a plural society in Britain is needed.

- Publicly funded institutions of higher education and their staff need to connect more closely with Muslim institutions.

- As issues relating to the future of Islamic Studies assume greater importance, both on university campuses and in the areas of funding and public policy, it is important to take account of, and respond to the variety of, interests involved in this subject.[120]

However, whilst there has been greater emphasis on ensuring that Islamic Studies or Muslim Chaplaincy courses in UK higher educational institutes contain a focus on modern libertarian secular life, that doesn't necessary change the here and the now in respect of Imams. It is not necessarily feasible for all Imams to take time out and study in higher educational institutes that have a specific focus on modern pluralistic life. The Department for Communities and Local Government has proposed Continuing Professional Development (CPD) where Imams take charge of their own development through a cyclical process of reflection, planning, action and evaluation.[121] CPD on it's own allows the individual to have continuous reflective

---

[120] Communities and Local Government. (2010) The training and development of Muslim Faith Leaders. pp.51
[121] Ibid

learning, and this would be thoroughly recommended in any occupation.

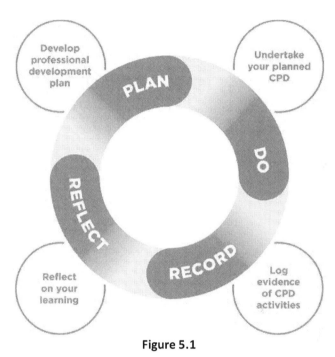

Figure 5.1

Continuing professional development

However, without monitoring, or making this a requirement of the role it leaves the opportunity for major variance in skillset amongst Imams. In simple terms, without making it mandatory, what is the incentive in an Imam engaging in CPD, and what is the consequence of not doing so? Most importantly CPD on its own, by its very nature will open inconsistencies in training where one Imam would potentially have done a lot more, or potentially a better quality CPD than another.

How is the congregant then aware as to which Imam is more suitably qualified and which one isn't? A more formal training approach is what I would therefore recommend.

Cognitive behavioural Therapy (CBT)

Various studies have shown that CBT on its own has been known to be efficacious in the treatment of mental health conditions such as Depression.[122] However Intervention studies have found that integrating religious beliefs in therapy has far more positive outcomes on religious clients than CBT therapy on its own.[123] Moreover, 77% to 83% of patients over age 55 wish to have their religious beliefs integrated into therapy.[124] A key recommendation in terms of training Imams would the availability of and access to Religiously Integrated CBT training. Religiously integrated CBT (RCBT) follows the same principles as conventional CBT, though a faith leader (in our case an Imam) would be trained on RCBT to listen to and support the client with a 'third ear.'[125] The major tools in RCBT (that are different to CBT) are the following:

---

[122] Hofmann, S. G., Asnaani, A., Vonk, I. J., Sawyer, A. T., & Fang, A. (2012) The Efficacy of Cognitive Behavioral Therapy: A Review of Meta-analyses. Cognitive therapy and research, 36(5), 427–440.
[123] Pearce, Michelle & Koenig, Harold & Robins, Clive & Nelson, Bruce & Shaw, Sally & Cohen, Harvey & King, Michael. (2014). Religiously Integrated Cognitive Behavioral Therapy: A New Method of Treatment for Major Depression in Patients With Chronic Medical Illness. Psychotherapy (Chicago, Ill.)
[124] Ibid. pp.3
[125] Ibid.

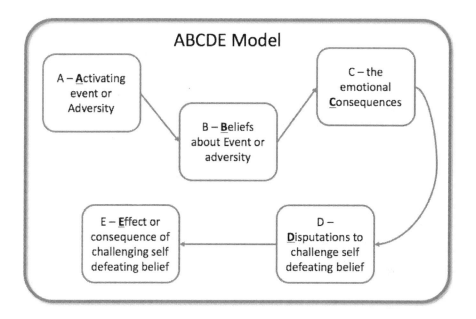

Figure 5.2

ABCDE Model

i.   Challenging one's thoughts using religious resources

Utilising Albert Ellis's ABCDE method (see below and footnote),[126] the practitioner helps the client identify unhelpful or negative thoughts, and by utilisation of scripture helps develop a pathway to a effective new belief with new Emotional and behavioural consequences (The E in ABCDE).[127]

---

[126] ICA. (2014) Rational Emotive Behavioral Approach and the ABCDE Model. [ONLINE] Available at: https://coachcampus.com/coach-portfolios/research-papers/monica-matei-rational-emotive-behavioral-approach-and-the-abcde-model [Accessed 08/08/20]
[127] Pearce, Michelle & Koenig, Harold & Robins, Clive & Nelson, Bruce & Shaw, Sally & Cohen, Harvey & King, Michael. (2014). pp.4

ii.   Religious practices

As part of the process to exact positive behavioural change clients are instructed to engage in several specific religious practices daily, such as contemplative prayer, scripture memorisation, as well as praying for others.[128]

iii.   Resources and community support

Away from the personal sessions clients are given resource material and are encouraged to spend time in comfortable environments for them within the community. This could be the mosque.

Whilst the above presents a generalised overview of what RCBT could look like practically, there needs to be a further study in to developing and piloting such a programme within Muslim communities. In a report on access to talking therapies (2013) produced by the charity MIND, the Royal College of Psychiatrists, and other affiliated groups showed that:

-     One in 10 people had been waiting over a year to receive CBT treatment.
-     Over half had been waiting over three months to receive treatment.
-     Around 13 per cent of people were still waiting for their first assessment for psychological therapy 28 days after referral.[129]

---

[128] Ibid. pp 5

[129] MIND. (2013) We still need to talk. A report on access to talking therapies. [ONLINE] Available at:https://psychoanalytic-council.org/media/494424/we-still-need-to-talk_report.pdf [Accessed 08/08/20]

In the last few years access to therapists has worsened leading to the NHS moving to computerised CBT (cCBT) where possible.[130] However these online modules have proven to be far from efficacious, and show no difference in patient outcomes as compared to normal medical treatment by the GP.[131]

The King's fund report into forecasting the cost of mental illness to the NHS by 2026 showed that untreated Depression can bring about further co-morbidities, and even death. The implications of untreated Depression could cost the NHS up to an additional £9 million per year.[132] Investing in psychological therapies such as CBT on untreated cases could save the NHS up to £16 million per year.[133] In its Mental health Implementation Plan (published 2019), the Department of Health and Social Care has committed to ringfencing a local investment fund worth at least £2.3 billion a year in real terms by 2023/24 and will ensure that the NHS provides high quality, evidence-based mental health services to an additional 2 million people.[134]

---

[130] NHS. (2020) Computerised Cognitive Behavioural Therapy (cCBT) – online psychological therapy. [ONLINE] Available at: https://www.cntw.nhs.uk/services/first-step/what-does-first-step-offer/ccbt/ [Accessed 08/08/20]

[131] The BMJ. (2015) Computerised cognitive behaviour therapy (cCBT) as treatment for depression in primary care (REEACT trial): large scale pragmatic randomised controlled trial. [ONLINE] Available at: https://www.bmj.com/content/351/bmj.h5627 [Accessed 08/08/20]

[132] King's Fund. (2008) PAYING THE PRICE The cost of mental health care in England to 2026. [ONLINE] Available at: https://www.kingsfund.org.uk/sites/default/files/Paying-the-Price-the-cost-of-mental-health-care-England-2026-McCrone-Dhanasiri-Patel-Knapp-Lawton-Smith-Kings-Fund-May-2008_0.pdf. pp 17 [Accessed 08/08/20]

[133] Ibid

[134] NHS. (2019) NHS Mental Health Implementation Plan 2019/20-2023/24. [ONLINE] Available at: https://www.longtermplan.nhs.uk/wp-content/uploads/2019/07/nhs-mental-health-implementation-plan-2019-20-2023-24.pdf [Accessed 08/08/20]

Partner organisations to the NHS such Public Health England could utilise this income as a great opportunity to follow on from their initial recommendations to involve faith leaders by piloting, and then developing RCBT training for Imams that wish to specialise in mental health support for congregants.[135] This in turn will not only lead to better patient outcomes but will also provide cost savings for the NHS long term (see King's Fund report).

Involving Muslim women

The data suggests a clear need for Muslim women to benefit from the spiritual support that is clearly more readily available for men. Our Imams showed a clear appetite for that, and some stated that an increased online presence such as virtual consultations with trained Imams online would be a step forward in providing that support. However, Muslim women may still see this as a barrier, as many would perhaps prefer speaking to female trained Aalimas.[136] Islamic seminary trained Muslim women work in various roles such as 'Chaplains in institutions such as hospitals, prisons and higher education, as scholars, thinkers and academics; as teachers and instructors in madrassahs and study circles, and in independent and state-funded Muslim schools, and in the management of mosques, often through a special women's committee.'[137] Thus it is important that Muslim women faith leaders are also offered the opportunity to train as specialists in RCBT therapy (thus **must** be included as part of a future

[135] The Mental Health Taskforce (2016)
[136] Communities and Local Government. (2010) The training and development of Muslim Faith Leaders. pp. 30
[137] Ibid

plan) opening up the opportunity for Muslim women in the community to get direct access and support from Aalima's and such alike.

A protocol for referral

The UK has strict safeguarding protocol for schools and institutions to highlight the abuse of children and vulnerable adults.[138] Referral protocols include the following:

- Ensuring that a safeguarding policy is in place and reviewed regularly
- A safeguarding lead is in place at the institution (child protection officer)
- Contact the local child protection/vulnerable adults team with specific details around the case for them to proceed further (bearing in mind the patients right to anonymity if they wish to do so).
- The safeguarding team will then decide on the provision of services. Information and advice.[139]

My recommendation is that as part of a pilot on (RCBT) a proper referral process is set up between practitioners similar to the already established safeguarding protocols in mosques. Our analysis shows that in theory if a protocol was in place, more referrals would take

---

[138] Diversity and equality in healthcare. (2020) Safeguarding children in madrassahs: a way forward. [ONLINE] Available at :
https://diversityhealthcare.imedpub.com/safeguarding-children-in-madrassahs-a-way-forward.php?aid=1901 [Accessed 08/08/20]
[139] Ibid

place. The NHS already has a simple referral system between practitioners that is online and provides professionals with an opportunity to request and respond to concerns.[140] My recommendation is that the e-Referral service is opened up for Imams that are trained in RCBT, and this would then form part of a formal referral process (bearing in mind patient consent beforehand).

I believe that the recommendations set out on the basis of the knowledge gained in this study show a clear appetite and way forward for Imams to play a central role in the mental health needs of their congregants, specifically in relation to Depression. I believe that a larger qualitative study would be needed nationwide to see whether the appetite is similar, and if so the next steps would be in setting up a pilot study based on the three keys recommendations suggested:

1. Provide formal RCBT training to Imams
2. Improve access for Muslim women to support through virtual sessions and RCBT trained Aalima's
3. Design a protocol of referral based on learnings from safeguarding policies and the e-Referral service to improve cross-sector collaboration.

---

[140] See eRS. [ONLINE] Available at: https://digital.nhs.uk/services/e-referral-service/document-library/advice-and-guidance-toolkit

Appendices

Figure/Graph	Title
1.1	PHE, Local suicide prevention planning, 2016
2.1	Literature review
3.1	Time, Resources, and Scope
3.2	Interview timings
3.3	Semi structured interview questions
3.4	Flowchart of how contact was made with Imams
4.1	Quantitative data analysis
4.2	Reasons for depressive illness
4.3	Identifying signs and symptoms of Depression
4.4	Jinn possession
4.5	Women and Access
4.6	Contacting other professionals
5.1	Continuing professional development
5.2	ABCDE Model

Appendix A – Information letter to Imams

Mohammed Kolia

XXXXXXXXXX

XXXXXXXXXX

XXXXXXXXX

TEL XXXXX XXX XXX

EMAIL XXXXXXXXXXXXXXXXX

Date XX/XX/XX

Research title: ***Identification and recognition of amongst Imams in Leicester, with special reference to creating a pathway of combined cross-sector care.***

Researcher: Mohammed Owaise Kolia

Supervisor name: Dr Zahid Parvez

Dear XXXXXXXXXXX

Assalamulaikum Wa rahmatullahi wa barakatuh,

My name is Mohammed Owaise. I am currently studying a Masters degree in Islamic studies at the Markfield Institute. As part of my dissertation I am researching the impact that Imams can have on tackling the mental health issues that are prevalent within our community. The hope is to understand whether a cross sector approach to care can be established with care professionals and

Imams to provide better outcomes for those suffering with Depression, and those that are supporting people through it.

I would like your consent to interview you in an audio recorded interview which will take place over the phone. I would be incredibly grateful for your participation in this very important study.

If you are happy to take part, please:

- **Read and sign the consent form attached and send back to me in the prepaid envelope provided or scanned and sent back to my email.**

Once I have received back your forms, we will then agree on an interview date and time. You will be emailed or messaged 24 hours before the interview date to confirm that you are still happy to go ahead.

The interview will follow General Data Protection guidelines, and the recording will be immediately deleted upon completion of the research. As part of the GDPR guidelines you will:
- Have the right to be informed
- The right of access to your data
- The right to rectification of your data
- The right to erasure of your data
- The right to restrict processing of your data
- The right to data portability

- The right to object
- Rights in relation to automated decision making and profiling

Should you have any queries with regards to how your data will be handled, or any queries in relation to the research please do not hesitate to contact me.

Many thanks

Mohammed Owaise Kolia

Appendix B – Consent form

Research title: *Identification and recognition of amongst Imams in Leicester, with special reference to creating a pathway of combined cross-sector care.*

Researcher: Mohammed Owaise Kolia

Supervisor name: Dr Zahid Parvez

1.   I confirm that I have read and understand the information sheet dated ………………for the above study and have had the opportunity to ask questions

2.   I understand that my participation is voluntary and that I am free to withdraw at any time/up until commencement of data analysis,
without giving any reason.

3.   I understand that my data will be stored securely and confidentially and that I will not be identifiable in any report or publication

4.   I understand that the researcher may wish to publish this study and any results found, for which I give my permission

5.   I agree for my interview to be audio recorded and for the data to be used for the purpose of this study.

6.   I agree to take part in the above study.

………………………….   ……………………….   ………………………….
Name   Date   Signature

………………………….   ……………………….   ………………………….
Name of person taking   Date   Signature
consent (if different from researcher, state position)

………………………….   ……………………….   ………………………….
Researcher   Date   Signature

Appendix C – Closed questions

Interviewee reference code   _____

Your Gender:

MALE	FEMALE

What would be your primary language(s) of communication with the community? (in order of use)

1
2
3

Your age group:

Below 25	25 to 39
40 to 60	60+

Years of experience as an Imam:

Less than 5 years	5 to 10 years
10 to 20 years	20 years plus

How long have you been in this country?

Born here	5 to 10 years
10 to 20 years	20 years plus

Was you all of your Islamic Education in this country?

Yes	No	In part

Please state and (non)vocational courses/higher education/post graduate courses studied in addition to Islamic education:

Does your mosque identify with a religious affiliation? If so, which one?

YES	NO	PREFER NOT TO SAY

How much of your time each week (approximately) is dedicated to meeting the counselling needs of your community (for depression related issues)?

ZERO HOURS	
1 -3 hours	6-9 hours
4-6 hours	9 hours +

How many hours a week do you work on average?

Less than 10	10 – 20
20 – 30	30 +

How many times on average in the last 12 months have you contacted the following for any of your congregants?

General practitioner (GP)	Zero	1 to 5	6-10	11-20	20 +
Social Worker	Zero	1 to 5	6-10	11-20	20 +
Family counsellor	Zero	1 to 5	6-10	11-20	20 +
Another Imam	Zero	1 to 5	6-10	11-20	20 +
Phychiatrist/ Psychologist	Zero	1 to 5	6-10	11-20	20 +
Consultant	Zero	1 to 5	6-10	11-20	20 +
Emergency services (111)	Zero	1 to 5	6-10	11-20	20 +
Other Professional(s) (please state)					

Appendix E – Semi structured open questions

Interviewee reference code_____

Phase 2 (10 mins)

In your opinion how often would you be in contact with people with depressive symptoms? (Discuss if problem is rising, why? and whether the Imam gets contacted by males and females)

Do you feel that it is easy or difficult to establish if someone has Depression?

Do you think there is a stigma around discussing mental health in the Muslim community, and where do you think that comes from? (10 mins) Do you think Jinn possession can be the cause of some cases of Depression?

Phase 3 Training and support (10 mins)

Do you think Imams are well equipped to deal with these issues? (Discuss if any additional issues)

In your view are Imams/should Imams be the first port of call for the community?

Do you feel that training and support (say on counselling) would equip you better to tackle these issues?

Phase 4 Reporting and referral (10 mins)

Have you had to report any safeguarding issues in the past to a vulnerable adults board children's safeguarding?

How you been involved actively on any occasions with other practitioners on the health and well being of a particular individuals(s)? What did this look like?

Do you feel Imams are given enough information on referral pathways? Or could they benefit from forming a part of that?

Phase 5 Additional comments (5mins)

Do you have any furthers comments to add? How do you see Depression and other related mental health issues developing in the future within the Muslim community? (Are things getting better or worse?)

Works cited

Al-Adawi, S., Dorvlo, A. S., Al-Ismaily, S. S., & et al. (2002) Perception of and attitude towards mental illness in Oman. The International Journal of Social Psychiatry, Volume 48, pp.305-317.

Ali O.M. Milstein, G. Marzuk P.M. (2005) The Imam's role in meeting the counselling needs of Muslim communities in the United States. [ONLINE] Available at: doi:10.1176/appi.ps.56.2.202 [Accessed 20/08/20]

Ali, M, O. Milstein, G. (2012) Journal of Muslim Mental health: Mental Illness Recognition and Referral Practices Among Imams in the United States. Michigan, USA: Michigan Publishing, Volume 6, Issue 2.

Al-Hilli, A. (1928) Al-Bābu al-hadi 'ashar. English translation by W. M. Miller. London, UK: Royal Asiatic Society, pp.392.

Al-Ashqar, Umar S. (2003) The World of the Jinn and Devils in the Light of the Qur'an and Sunnah. UK: International Islamic Publishing House.

Aloud, N., & Rathur, A. (2009) Factors affecting attitudes towards seeking and using formal mental health and psychological services among Arab Muslim populations. Journal of Muslim Mental Health, 4, 79-103. [ONLINE] Available at: http://dx.doi. org/10.1080/15564900802487675 [Accessed 03/02/20]

At-Tabari, I.J. (2000) Jami' al-Bayan fi Ta'wil al-Qur'an. Translated by Michael Fishbein. Los Angeles, USA: State University of New York Press.

Badri, M. (2013) Abu Zayd al-Balkhi's sustenance of the soul the cognitive behaviour therapy of a ninth century physician. Herndon, USA: the international institute of Islamic thought.

BACP. (2018) Ethical Guidelines for Research in the Counselling Professions. [ONLINE] Available at: https://www.bacp.co.uk/media/3908/bacp-ethical-guidelines-for-research-counselling-professions.pdf [Accessed 14/12/19]

BERA. (2018) Ethical guidelines for educational research. [ONLINE] Available at: https://www.bera.ac.uk/researchers-resources/publications/ethical-guidelines-for-educational-research-2018 [Accessed 14/12/19]

Ciftci, A. Jones, N. Corrigan, P. (2012) Journal of Muslim Mental health: Mental health stigma in the Muslim community. Michigan, USA: Michigan Publishing, Volume 7, Issue 1, pp. 17-31.

Communities and Local Government. (2010) The training and development of Muslim Faith Leaders. [ONLINE] Available at: https://assets.publishing.service.gov.uk/government/uploads/system/uploads/attachment_data/file/6155/1734121.pdf, pp. 30, [Accessed 01/10/2019]

Deacon, B. (2013) The biomedical model of mental disorder: A critical analysis of its validity, utility, and effects on psychotherapy research. Clinical Psychology Review. [ONLINE] Available at: https://jonabram.web.unc.edu/files/2013/09/Deacon_biomedical_mo del_2013.pdf [Accessed 01/10/19]

DHSC. (2020) Prime Minister's statement on coronavirus (COVID-19): 23 March 2020
[ONLINE] Available at:
https://www.gov.uk/government/speeches/pm-address-to-the-nation-on-coronavirus-23-march-2020 [Accessed 01/08/20]

DHSC. (2020) Meeting people from outside your household: guidance for Leicester [ONLINE] Available at:
https://www.gov.uk/government/publications/local-lockdown-guidance-for-social-distancing/meeting-people-from-outside-your-household-guidance-for-leicester [Accessed 20/08/20]

Diversity and equality in healthcare. (2020) Safeguarding children in madrassahs: a way forward. [ONLINE] Available at :
https://diversityhealthcare.imedpub.com/safeguarding-children-in-madrassahs-a-way-forward.php?aid=1901 [Accessed 08/08/20]

Eaton, N. (2015) Hijab, Religiosity, and Psychological Wellbeing of Muslim Women in the United States. Journal of Muslim Mental Health. USA: Michigan Publishing, Volume 9, issue 2

Given, L. (editor) (2008) The Sage encyclopaedia of qualitative research methods. Volume 2. California, USA: Sage publications.

Gulliver, A. Griffiths, K. (2010) Perceived barriers and facilitators to mental health help-seeking in young people: a systematic review. BMC Pshyciatry. [ONLINE] Available at: https://bmcpsychiatry.biomedcentral.com/track/pdf/10.1186/1471-244X-10-113 [Accessed 13/03/20]

Gutas, D. (1997) Greek thought, Arabic culture. London, UK: Taylor and Francis group.

HM Government Department of Health and Social Care. (2017) Preventing Suicide in England: Third progress report of the cross-government outcomes strategy to save lives. [ONLINE] Available at https://assets.publishing.service.gov.uk/government/uploads/system/uploads/attachment_data/file/582117/Suicide_report_2016_A.pdf [Accessed 01/10/19]

Hofmann, S. G., Asnaani, A., Vonk, I. J., Sawyer, A. T., & Fang, A. (2012) The Efficacy of Cognitive Behavioral Therapy: A Review of Meta-analyses. Cognitive therapy and research, 36(5), 427–440. Information Commissioner's office (2020) Individual rights. [ONLINE] Available at: https://ico.org.uk/for-organisations/guide-to-data-protection/guide-to-the-general-data-protection-regulation gdpr/individual-rights [Accessed 01/08/20]

Hofmann, S. G., Asnaani, A., Vonk, I. J., Sawyer, A. T., & Fang, A. (2012) The Efficacy of Cognitive Behavioural Therapy: A Review of Meta-analyses. Cognitive therapy and research, 36(5), pp. 427–440.

ICA. (2014) Rational Emotive Behavioral Approach and the ABCDE Model. [ONLINE] Available at: https://coachcampus.com/coach-portfolios/research-papers/monica-matei-rational-emotive-behavioral-approach-and-the-abcde-model/ [Accessed 08/08/20]

ICD-10. (2010) [ONLINE] Available at https://icd.who.int/browse10/2010/en#/F32 [Accessed 20/08/20]

Jorm, A. (2011). Mental Health Literacy: Empowering the Community to Take Action for Better Mental Health. American Psychologist. [ONLINE] Available at: https://www.semanticscholar.org/paper/Mental-health-literacy%3A-empowering-the-community-to-Jorm/69946b3064897c38d27596d2c4902f431f0dbb67 [Accessed 01/10/19]

Joseph Rowntree Foundation (2011). The impact of the global economic downturn on communities and poverty in the UK. [ONLINE] Available at https://www.jrf.org.uk/report/impact-global-economic-downturn-communities-and-poverty-uk [Accessed 01/10/19]

Khalifa, N, Hardie, T, Mullick. (2012) Jinn and Psychiatry: Comparison of Beliefs among Muslims in Dhaka and Leicester. Publications Archive: Royal College of Psychiatrists' Spirituality and Psychiatry Special Interest Group, [ONLINE] Available at: http://www.rcpsych.ac.uk/workinpsychiatry/specialinterestgroups/spirituality/publicationsarchive.aspxk). [Accessed 20/08/20]

Lim, A., Hoek, H. W., Ghane, S., Deen, M., & Blom, J. D. (2018) The Attribution of Mental Health Problems to Jinn: An Explorative Study in a Transcultural Psychiatric Outpatient Clinic. *Frontiers in psychiatry*, *9*, 89. [ONLINE] Available at: https://doi.org/10.3389/fpsyt.2018.00089 [Accessed 20/08/20]

Losing the mind. (2003) Los Angeles Times. [ONLINE] Available at: https://www.latimes.com/archives/la-xpm-2003-oct-26-tm-survivors43-story.html [Accessed 01/10/19]

Mars, B., Heron, J., Kessler, D., Davies, N. M., Martin, R. M., Thomas, K. H., & Gunnell, D. (2017) Influences on antidepressant prescribing trends in the UK: 1995-2011. Social psychiatry and psychiatric epidemiology, 52(2), pp. 193–200

MCB (2015). Terrorists cannot divide us. [ONLINE] Available at: https://mcb.org.uk/general/unity-home-meeting-160115/ [Accessed 14/12/19]

Mental health effects of school closures during COVID-19. (2020) Available [ONLINE] at:

https://www.thelancet.com/journals/lanchi/article/PIIS2352-4642(20)30109-7/fulltext [Accessed 01/06/2020]

MIND (2013) We still need to talk. A report on access to talking therapies. [ONLINE] Available at:https://psychoanalytic-council.org/media/494424/we-still-need-to-talk_report.pdf [Accessed 08/08/20]

Mir, G. (2014). Adapted behavioural activation for the treatment of depression in Muslims. [ONLINE] Available at: http://medhealth.leeds.ac.uk/info/615/research/327/addressing_depr ession_in_muslim_communities [Accessed 13/12/19]

Muslims in Britain (2018). Mosques in Leicestershire. [ONLINE] Available at: https://mosques.muslimsinbritain.org/maps.php#/town/Leicester [Accessed 14/12/19]

Nabolsi, M. M., & Carson, A. M. (2011) Spirituality, illness, and personal responsibility: The experience of Jordanian Muslim men with coronary artery disease. Scandinavian Journal of Caring Sciences, 25, pp.716-724.

Namey, Emily & Guest, Greg & Thairu, Lucy. (2008). Data reduction techniques for large qualitative data sets. California, USA: Sage publications.

National Institute for Health and Care Excellence. (2009) Depression in Adults: Recognition and Management. [ONLINE] Available at https://www.nice.org.uk/guidance/cg90/resources/depression-in-adults-recognition-and-management-pdf-975742638037 [Accessed 13/12/19]

National Institute for Health and Care Excellence. (2020) Antidepressant drugs. [ONLINE] Available at: https://bnf.nice.org.uk/treatment-summary/antidepressant-drugs.html [Accessed 01/03/20]

Newcomer, K. Hatry, H. Wholey, J. (2015) Handbook of practical program evaluation. 4th edition. Jersey, USA: Joh Wiley & Sons inc. pp 27

NHS Digital. (2017) Antidepressants were the area with largest increase in prescription items in 2016. [ONLINE] Available at: https://digital.nhs.uk/news-and-events/news-archive/2017-news-archive/antidepressants-were-the-area-with-largest-increase-in-prescription-items-in-2016 [Accessed 01/10/19]

NHS. (2020) Computerised Cognitive Behavioural Therapy (cCBT) – online psychological therapy. [ONLINE] Available at: https://www.cntw.nhs.uk/services/first-step/what-does-first-step-offer/ccbt/ [Accessed 08/08/20]

NHS. (2019) NHS Mental Health Implementation Plan 2019/20-2023/24. [ONLINE] Available at: https://www.longtermplan.nhs.uk/wp-content/uploads/2019/07/nhs-mental-health-implementation-plan-2019-20-2023-24.pdf [Accessed 08/08/20]

Pearce, Michelle & Koenig, Harold & Robins, Clive & Nelson, Bruce & Shaw, Sally & Cohen, Harvey & King, Michael. (2014). Religiously Integrated Cognitive Behavioral Therapy: A New Method of Treatment for Major Depression in Patients With Chronic Medical Illness. Psychotherapy (Chicago, Ill.)

Psychology today. (2013) ADHD and the Problem of the Double Hermeneutic. [ONLINE] Available at: https://www.psychologytoday.com/gb/blog/theory-knowledge/201312/adhd-and-the-problem-the-double-hermeneutic [Accessed 22/03/2020]

Public Health England. (2016) Local Suicide prevention planning. [ONLINE] Available at: https://assets.publishing.service.gov.uk/government/uploads/system/uploads/attachment_data/file/585411/PHE_local_suicide_prevention _planning_practice_resource.pdf. pp.16 [Accessed 01/10/19]

Public Health England. (2018) Suicide prevention profile. [ONLINE] Available at https://fingertips.phe.org.uk/profile/suicide/data#page/0/gid/193813

2828/pat/6/par/E12000004/ati/102/are/E06000016 [Accessed 01/10/19]

Rahman, S. Ahmed, S. Khan, S. (2006) Voices from the minarets: MCB study of UK imams and mosques. Stratford, UK: Published by The Muslim Council of Britain.

Rassool, G. H. (2018) Evil Eye, Jinn Possession, and Mental Health Issues: An Islamic Perspective (Explorations in Mental Health). Oxon, UK: Routledge.

Rethink mental illness (2020) Depression. [ONLINE] Available at: https://www.rethink.org/advice-and-information/about-mental-illness/learn-more-about-conditions/depression/ [Accessed 20/08/20]

Revealed: Massive rise in antidepressant prescribing. (2019) RTE. [ONLINE] Available at: https://www.rte.ie/news/investigations-unit/2019/0218/1031271-massive-rise-antidepressant-prescribing/ [Accessed 01/03/20]

Sabry, W. Vohra, A. (2013) Role of Islam in the management of Psychiatric disorders. Indian Journal of Psychiatry. [ONLINE] Available at: https://www.ncbi.nlm.nih.gov/pmc/articles/PMC3705684/?report=printable#ref5 [Accessed 13/12/19]

Saldana, J. (2013) The coding manual for qualitative researchers. Los Angeles, USA: SAGE Publications.

Samaritans. (2019) Suicide statistics report. [ONLINE] Available at: https://www.samaritans.org/documents/402/SamaritansSuicideStatsReport_2019_AcMhRyF.pdf. [Accessed 01/10/19]

Saunders, M., Lewis, P. & Thornhill, A. (2012) Research Methods for Business Students. 6th edition. UK: Pearson Education Limited

Sulaymān ibn al-Ash'ath, A, D. (2008) Sunan Abu Dawud. English Translation. New York: Darussalam International publications. Volume 4.

The BMJ. (2015) Computerised cognitive behaviour therapy (cCBT) as treatment for depression in primary care (REEACT trial): large scale pragmatic randomised controlled trial. [ONLINE] Available at: https://www.bmj.com/content/351/bmj.h5627 [Accessed 08/08/20]

The Guardian. (2018) Bank of England says no-deal Brexit would be worse than 2008 crisis.
[ONLINE] Available at:
https://www.theguardian.com/business/2018/nov/28/bank-of-england-says-no-deal-brexit-would-be-worse-than-2008-crisis [Accessed 01/12/19]

The Mental Health Taskforce. (2016) The Five Year Forward View for Mental Health: A report from the independent Mental Health Taskforce to the NHS in England. [ONLINE] Available at:

https://www.england.nhs.uk/wp-content/uploads/2016/02/Mental-Health-Taskforce-FYFV-final.pdf [Accessed 01/10/19]

King's Fund. (2008) PAYING THE PRICE The cost of mental health care in England to 2026. [ONLINE] Available at: https://www.kingsfund.org.uk/sites/default/files/Paying-the-Price-the-cost-of-mental-health-care-England-2026-McCrone-Dhanasiri-Patel-Knapp-Lawton-Smith-Kings-Fund-May-2008_0.pdf. pp 17 [Accessed 08/08/20]

Thomas, F. Hansford, L. Ford, J. Wyatt, K. McCabe, R. & Byng, R. (2019) How accessible and acceptable are current GP referral mechanisms for IAPT for low-income patients? Lay and primary care perspectives, Journal of Mental Health, DOI: 10.1080/09638237.2019.1677876 [Accessed 03/02/20]

Tibi S. (2006). Al-Razi and Islamic medicine in the 9th century. Journal of the Royal Society of Medicine, 99(4), 206–207. https://doi.org/10.1258/jrsm.99.4.206 [Accessed 01/10/19]

Trivedi J. K. (2006). Cognitive deficits in psychiatric disorders: Current status. Indian journal of psychiatry, 48(1),

Tzeferakos, G.A., Douzenis, A.I. (2017) Islam, mental health and law: a general overview. Ann Gen Psychiatry 16, 28. [ONLINE] Available at: https://doi.org/10.1186/s12991-017-0150-6 Accessed [12/02/20]

Tucker, K. (1998) Anthony Giddens and modern social theory. New York, USA: Sage publications.

Walsham, G. (1995) The Emergence of Interpretivism in IS Research. Information Systems Research, 6(4), 376-394. [ONLINE] Available at: www.jstor.org/stable/23010981 [Accessed 01/10/2019]

Weatherhead, S. Davies, A. (2010) Muslim views on mental health and psychotherapy: The British Psychological Society. [ONLINE] Available at https://www.researchgate.net/publication/26794589_Muslim_views_on_mental_health_and_psychotherapy. [Accessed 13/12/19]

Whiteford, H. Ferrari, A. et al. (2010) The Global Burden of Mental, Neurological and Substance Use Disorders: An Analysis from the Global Burden of Disease Study. [ONLINE] Available online at: https://journals.plos.org/plosone/article?id=10.1371/journal.pone.0116820 [Accessed 13/03/20]

Yin, R. K. (2003) Case study research: Design and methods, 3rd edition. California, USA: Sage publications, pp.16

Bibliography

Ali O.M. Milstein, G. Marzuk P.M. (2005) The Imam's role in meeting the counselling needs of Muslim communities in the United

States. [ONLINE] Available at: doi:10.1176/appi.ps.56.2.202 [Accessed 20/08/20]

Al-Ashqar, Umar S. (2003) The World of the Jinn and Devils in the Light of the Qur'an and Sunnah. UK: International Islamic Publishing House.

Joseph Rowntree Foundation (2011). The impact of the global economic downturn on communities and poverty in the UK. [ONLINE] Available at https://www.jrf.org.uk/report/impact-global-economic-downturn-communities-and-poverty-uk [Accessed 01/10/19]

Khalifa, N, Hardie, T, Mullick. (2012) Jinn and Psychiatry: Comparison of Beliefs among Muslims in Dhaka and Leicester. Publications Archive: Royal College of Psychiatrists' Spirituality and Psychiatry Special Interest Group, [ONLINE] Available at: http://www.rcpsych.ac.uk/workinpsychiatry/specialinterestgroups/spirituality/publicationsarchive.aspxk). [Accessed 20/08/20]

Lim, A., Hoek, H. W., Ghane, S., Deen, M., & Blom, J. D. (2018) The Attribution of Mental Health Problems to Jinn: An Explorative Study in a Transcultural Psychiatric Outpatient Clinic. Frontiers in psychiatry, 9, 89. [ONLINE] Available at: https://doi.org/10.3389/fpsyt.2018.00089 [Accessed 20/08/20]

MIND (2013) We still need to talk. A report on access to talking therapies. [ONLINE] Available at:https://psychoanalytic-council.org/media/494424/we-still-need-to-talk_report.pdf [Accessed 08/08/20]

Mir, G. (2014). Adapted behavioural activation for the treatment of depression in Muslims. [ONLINE] Available at: http://medhealth.leeds.ac.uk/info/615/research/327/addressing_depr ession_in_muslim_communities [Accessed 13/12/19]

Samaritans. (2019) Suicide statistics report. [ONLINE] Available at: https://www.samaritans.org/documents/402/SamaritansSuicideStatsR eport_2019_AcMhRyF.pdf. [Accessed 01/10/19]

Saunders, M., Lewis, P. & Thornhill, A. (2012) Research Methods for Business Students. 6th edition. UK: Pearson Education Limited

The Mental Health Taskforce. (2016) The Five Year Forward View for Mental Health: A report from the independent Mental Health Taskforce to the NHS in England. [ONLINE] Available at: https://www.england.nhs.uk/wp-content/uploads/2016/02/Mental-Health-Taskforce-FYFV-final.pdf [Accessed 01/10/19]

Yin, R. K. (2003) Case study research: Design and methods, 3rd edition. California, USA: Sage publications.

This page is intentionally left blank

Printed in Great Britain
by Amazon